UPROOTED

My Family's Journey from Starvation in Calcutta to Success in Trinidad

Zobi Fredrick

iUniverse, Inc.
Bloomington

UPROOTED

iUniverse books may be ordered through booksellers or by contacting:

iUniverse
1663 Liberty Drive
Bloomington, IN 47403
www.iuniverse.com
1-800-Authors (1-800-288-4677)

ISBN: 978-1-4401-4301-4 (sc)
ISBN: 978-1-4401-4302-1 (e)

Printed in the United States of America

iUniverse rev. date: 01/24/2013

TABLE OF CONTENTS

ACKNOWLEDGEMENTS

This is a work of nonfiction. The characters and events depicted in this book are real. They are my family. My deepest appreciation goes to my dear sister in London, Nisa Khan – lawyer, advisor, Civil Rights leader–for much of the materials and observations. My sister spent many hours painstakingly reading through the drafts. I also thank my dear friend Hank Gartland who helped with the editing. This book could not have been written without their support and assistance.

FAMILY TREE

Mohammed Moktee departed Calcutta, India on November 19, 1851 (Equestrian).
Arrived in Trinidad on March 17, 1852. Based on this information we begin our 'Family Tree'.

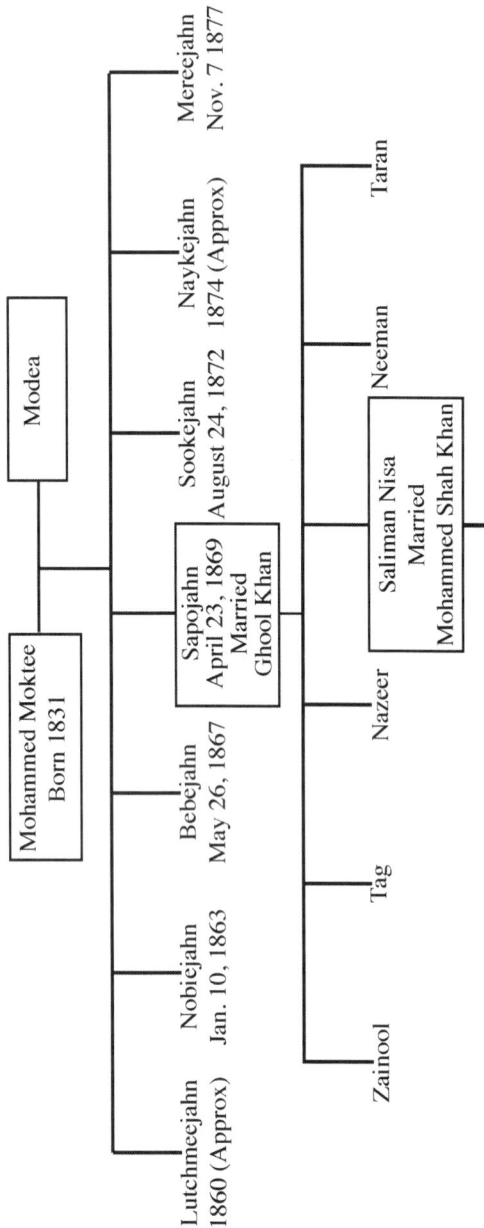

Mohammed Moktee Born 1831	Modea

- Lutchmeejahn 1860 (Approx)
- Nobiejahn Jan. 10, 1863
- Bebejahn May 26, 1867
- Sapojahn April 23, 1869 Married Ghool Khan
- Sookejahn August 24, 1872
- Naykejahn 1874 (Approx)
- Mereejahn Nov. 7 1877

Children of Sapojahn:
- Zainool
- Tag
- Nazeer
- Saliman Nisa Married Mohammed Shah Khan
- Neeman
- Taran

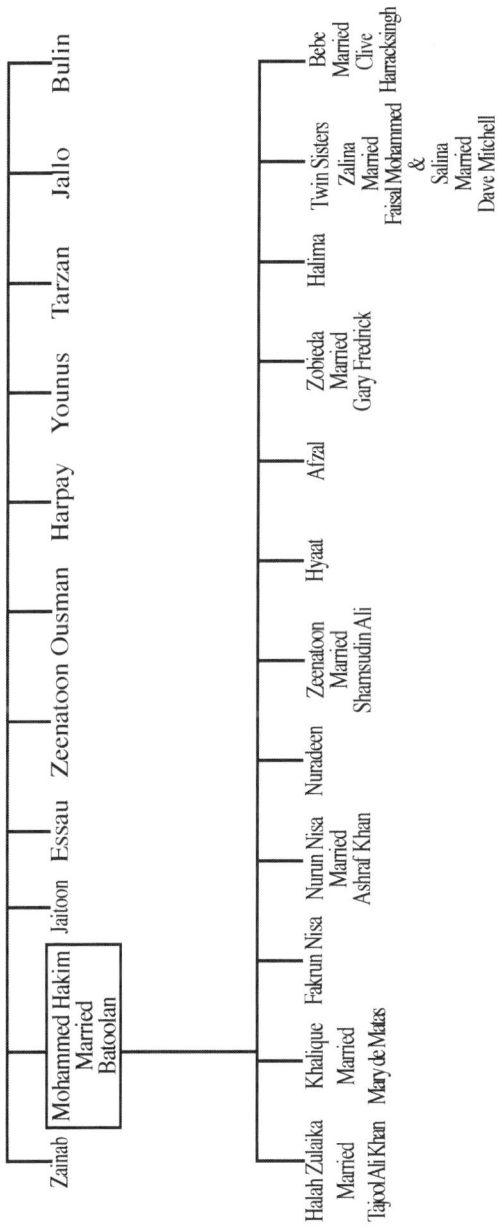

Family tree

Children of the first generation:
Zainab — Mohammed Hakim (Married Batoolan) — Jaitoon — Essau — Zeenatoon — Ousman — Harpay — Younus — Tarzan — Jallo — Bulin

Children of Mohammed Hakim (Married Batoolan):

- Halak Zulaika, Married Tajool Ali Khan
- Khalique, Married Mary de Matas
- Fakrun Nisa
- Nurun Nisa, Married Ashraf Khan
- Nuradeen
- Zeenatoon, Married Shamsudin Ali
- Hyaat
- Afzal
- Zobieda, Married Gary Fredrick
- Halima
- Twin Sisters: Zalina Married Faisal Mohammed & Salina Married Dave Mitchell
- Bebe, Married Clive Harracksingh

THE FAMILY PHOTOGRAPH

PREFACE

Conditions in India

Here is a story that is real and imaginative. It may be difficult for the modern reader to imagine what happened so many years ago. Indentured laborers were coming in desperation from their homeland in India in search of a better life and arriving on a small island on the other side of the world in the Caribbean. These people had few choices. This story shows real bravery, hardship, and dedication through which the poor yet fascinating Indian immigrants created their new lives in a new land.

Can you and I imagine what it was like in India during a famine? Starving people had no crops to harvest from the dry, barren land; and there were no cows to milk. Women and children were helpless because they could not get a decent meal. Cholera, dysentery, and outbreaks of other diseases, caused many to die miserably under those poor conditions. The only way out was to go to the new land--Trinidad: There they could work, get three meals a day, medical care and wages too. This seemed like being sent to heaven; after all, they were already in hell. So the poor workers signed five year contracts under the British indentured labor system. How could they resist such an offer? In India they surely would have died. With this offer from the British, they had a chance to work and become free laborers after five years - with the promised money in their pockets, to return home or to invest in whatever they chose to do. Seemingly, they could now have a goal. The need to have far better lives for themselves and their families was apparent and indeed the British contracts fulfilled that need. The people who came to the island of Trinidad from India during the days of indentureship came because of the terrible conditions at home, and the promise of a better future, but not because they were forced. There were no whips, chains, or jail cells. Most figured that they would work their five years and return with money of their own. They were having a great famine and many, many people - thousands - were going to die.

It would be a mistake to say that the Indians who came under the labor contract to Trinidad were beaten, whipped or kept in slave-like conditions. They certainly were not slaves. In fact, the British Empire had outlawed slavery. Although it is true that they came voluntarily, these people really had little choice. They went willingly to Trinidad (and other places within the British Empire) to become farm laborers rather than to stay home and slowly starve to death. Given a choice to live or die, they chose life. They believed that the work they were hired to do in the sugar plantations would not hurt or kill them. They were competent farm workers and were brought to Trinidad by the British government and the plantation owners. The owners considered the Indian laborers to be valuable "machines" used to produce sugar cane. Although they worked hard and lived in poor conditions, these conditions were better than living in the streets of Calcutta with no food or medical attention. In Trinidad, Indian workers were promised medical care, three meals a day, and a life under a British legal system which would protect even them from the worst abuses.

So with poverty, famine, and starvation certain if they were to remain; and with government contracts promising steady jobs along with food, housing, a small salary, medical care, and a free trip home at the end of the term, many saw this as an opportunity. Although these immigrants worked by the sweat of their brows without many complaints, when they arrived in Trinidad, they lived in poor conditions. But living in cramped barracks was better than living in a Calcutta street with no food at all. Here at least, they had breakfast, lunch and dinner, and they lived under the same British rule. They knew that in certain amounts, however small, the British legal system would protect them. The work they were assigned, although long and hard, was not designed to harm them.

Their labor was, after all, essential to the financial success of the plantations, and so they signed up voluntarily, even if under pressure at home in India. If too many laborers returned to India with tales of abuse, recruiting would be extremely difficult, so there was no incentive to treat the workers as slaves. In those days, difficult, dirty, and dangerous work was the rule for manual laborers, and these indentured workers from India seemed to get no more or no less than normal.

In spite of the fact that the Indians were indentured laborers and not slaves, they were not exactly "free" to leave the plantation on their own. They were required to fulfill their contracts. When they had fulfilled the terms of their indentureship, the laborers were allowed to return to India. Most were encouraged to sign up for another five years. Many found other work in Trinidad. The ones who stayed became taxi drivers, carpenters, shopkeepers, or farmers. Some even came to own real estate. The Indian indentured servants-turned-immigrants eventually became what is the Indian business community of Trinidad today. How did they do that? What qualities did they have? What kinds of skills did they possess? Quite basically, these men and women were self-taught people who had perseverance but no great education to bring with them. In India these people were poor, starving peasants, farmers who had not enough money to survive.

They came to Trinidad, a land which was completely alien to them. To a poor peasant farmer in impoverished Bihar, India, who never saw a body of water bigger than a river, who never saw an ocean, to get into a ship is the same as going in a spaceship to Mars. On this journey to the other end of the world, enduring a treacherous ocean voyage, some of these confused Indians had only a vague idea what they were signing up for. They were motivated by hunger. This journey to Trinidad was like another world: they felt frightened and confused. Imagine the fright that went through their minds aboard the ship, not knowing what to expect in going to an unknown land. They rolled, pitched, and lived among diseased rats, a hurricane at sea, bad food. And yet when they came to Trinidad, they worked hard.

Eventually, Indian laborers prospered and still prosper on that little island. They continue to dominate the Trinidad business world, to do whatever it takes, and to take control of businesses to get ahead in a poor land. Like birds of a feather, they stuck together and made good their lives by not only fulfilling their contracts, but also by their strength, will, and dignity. The struggle for survival in those harsh cane fields only encouraged them to prove themselves as worthy workers to the British overseers. For their work, they would receive a small sum of money at the end of the week. The indentured laborers usually saved their meager salaries and the money they received at the end of their contracts. With this, they could buy cows, farmland, or a small business; they finally were able to take care of their families in decent ways and also go further to pursue other industry. Looking back, my ancestors had jobs with little pay, but they saw that they had the ability to be independent if they worked hard. In India poverty and starvation had caused them to be at the bottom of the ladder, with little self value. But in Trinidad they showed the plantation overseers that they were capable of enduring what was given to them during the five-year contract. They were able to show, that they could rise above these difficult circumstances through dedication and hard work, if given the opportunity.

I imagine the satisfaction that my great, great grandfather must have felt when he finished his contract and was no longer obligated to the British who had always told him what to do and how to live his life. A free man at last! My ancestors had paved the road to success and transferred from one generation to the next their dreams of a whole new way of life. I, too, have acquired the will to pick up the pieces of what had taken place in a time when people lived in a hard cruel world crying out for a better life and eventually had so much more. I hope the reader will understand that I am relating a story that few outsiders can know. As a child I grew up with the history and culture of Trinidad and the true stories of a family passed down to tell of what happened to bring us to where we are today.

Now I am a mother, and I wish my parents were at my side. For this reason I am moved to record this brief history of my family and its odyssey…its dream of a better life and its struggle upward from the plantation where it all began.

INTRODUCTION

My name is Zobi Fredrick. I was born in Trinidad, and educated in London, where I was a successful fashion model. I married in the US, raised two children, studied acting and diction in New York City, and have had several small parts in film and television. This is my story but also the story of many Indians who, like so many other US immigrants, left their homelands to seek a better life. Let me start at the beginning.

FOREWORD

Zobi Fredrick has written this book, in hopes that it will do a great deal of good to people of all cultures and races. With the help of her sister and family members, she tells the story of her experiences. Much research and effort were put into this book. The author has depicted a story of one family's journey and of one man's struggle to follow his dream. This man took on a difficult task and gave everything to this goal, with all his wit and energy and even to the point of neglecting his own family. It is a tale of one man's contribution to the political and social conditions in his hometown, based on his strong religious feelings. His contributions to building a mosque for the Indian community to have a place of worship depicts, that Mohammed Hakim Khan, my father, wanted unification and had no biased feelings toward people of different races and cultures. All were equally welcome with open arms. I hope that you will find reading this manuscript as rewarding, alive as it has been written.

ILLUSTRATIONS

TRINIDAD MUSLIM LEAGUE   MOHAMMED HAKIM KHAN

"All praise is due to Allah the Lord of the Worlds, may His Blessings be on His Servant, Mohammed." (The opening chapter of the Holy Quaran).

The Jinnah Memorial Mosque was inaugurated on August 15th, 1947, at St. Joseph by a group of devoted Muslims led by Mr. Mohammed Hakim Khan, who was the first President of the Trinidad Muslim League. It was under the auspices of this organization and with Khan's leadership that the Mosque was finally completed at St. Joseph. He believed the Qur'ans injunction that: "The pen of the scholar is mightier than the sword of the warrior." Many thanks are due to his faithful friends for their support and dedication on this great achievement.

Chapter 1

IN THE BEGINNING

Bihar Tourist Map

Map not to Scale

Copyright © Indian Holiday Pvt. Ltd. 2006-07

Bihar

In the middle of the noise and confusion of the crowded marketplace Moktee was completely alone for the first time of his life. He came from a small town in the state of Bihar, a farmer, the son of a farmer but when the rains came and the floods came everything was washed away. He lost his mother. He lost his sister. That was two years ago. This year no rains came, the ground dried up. The winds blew the dust away and there were no crops. Everyone was hungry, his father and his brother died from diseases. Although he was only nineteen he had worked for almost ten years on the farms. He knew all about farming. He knew it was hard work. Now the farms were parched, there was no work, there was no food and he was all alone. After struggling alone with no one else for many months, maybe half a year, Moktee worked up the courage to ask an old man who lived in the village, a family friend for a small amount of money. He wanted to go, desirous to seek his fortune in the great city of Calcutta. He had heard so much about it. Surely the people in this city were not struggling like the people were in his little village. He would use his brains and his brawn to get himself a really good job in the great city and make lots of money and return a wealthy and successful man. It was not so hard really, he told himself, he was young and strong. Full of optimism about the future in spite of what had happened. So he packed up his belongings, a shirt, a prayer book, a bit of rice and headed for the market where he knew the vendors would be setting up for the following day and the bullock carts would be coming from all over with their supplies. Moktee had been to the market many times; it was always a pleasant occasion to buy supplies and food. This time it was different, he was hungry, he was tired, and he was soaking wet from the rain. This time he was a little more desperate, a little more hungry than usual. He had to make a connection with one of the bullock cart drivers. He would do anything, he would help them load and unload. Help them take care of the animals; feed them or whatever it took. He did anything just so that he could get a ride to another town and maybe from that town to the next town. Days and days it would take and he only had a little bit of money but he was a hard worker and that was his advantage.

He had really no idea how long it would take to get to the great city of Calcutta. He had no idea how tough it would be to ride those little carts on those rugged roads filled with potholes and ruts and mud and rocks You felt every one of those when you were sitting in the cart. Sometimes it was easier to get out and walk. Even a young strong man like Moktee could be battered and bruised at the end of several days in a bullock cart. It may even take a week, ten days or maybe two weeks. It was brutally hot and dusty. The precious monsoons they were waiting for so desperately, were supposed to come every year at the same time. This year they came, but they came too late.

Now there was mud everywhere and it rained for a good bit of the trip. It was miserable; sometimes he had to sleep under the cart.

After what seemed like months and months they came to a place where they could see the great city of Calcutta in the distance. In another day they would be there. He actually felt a little excitement and gathered up his courage. He was not very religious but he decided to say a prayer of thanksgiving. He knew he should and he did. Moktee had never seen or imagined in his wildest dreams anything like the city of Calcutta. It was so big and with so many people. He had never seen so many people in his life. There were so many sights, sounds, smells, shouting and yelling. People were talking in languages that he had never heard before. He did not even know there were foreign languages.

Moktee had spent the entire first day after his arrival in Calcutta going from vendor to vendor in the market looking for work that he could do. He was tired and frustrated. With very little work to be had, he was not able to get work right away. All he could find out was that because of the drought and the bad farming conditions there were many, many just like him who had come to the city to get work.

Many thousands of people out of work, hungry and homeless, with little to eat Sometimes there was very little to eat, sometimes nothing. Work was very hard to get. That one day without work stretched out to a week. A week with no work and almost nothing to eat and no money. Things were getting very desperate.

The next morning he got up before sunrise. He had nothing to eat. He went to the market to look for work and finally one of the vendors asked him to unload one of his wagons and set up his table. And so he had his first little bit of work. The vendor bought him a little bit of food to keep him strong. Moktee thought that this was the best food he had ever had. The work was hard and the little old man did not help. It was his business after all. It started to rain and Moktee continued to unload and set up. As the sun came up Moktee joined the man behind the table. He watched carefully as the man began to sell his wares, how he bargained for every item, how he tried to strike a fair bargain that would give him a bit of money and make the customer happy too. Moktee watched and listened and learned from this. At the end of the day Moktee had helped the man and then began to load the cart again.

The man thanked him, paid him a bit and said that he had done a good job and he would see him next week if Moktee was still around. Moktee thought "Next week! My gosh, again I am out of a job". What am I going to do for a whole week. I need to find something else to do in the meantime. At the end of the day Moktee was bruised, hurting in every muscle and exhausted but he was happy to have had this day of work in the big city although he had not expected it to be quite this hard to find work. After all, his mission was to come to the big city and find a job and make a lot of money as he had always heard you could do in the big city and return to his town a successful man. But it was already weeks and weeks into his mission and he had just now had his first day of work with no promise immediately of any future work. Moktee was intrigued however by the man that he worked for and the market that they were working in because of all the hustle, bustle, shouting and yelling, the bartering. There was a tremendous amount of excitement in the market and some of the vendors did appear to be wealthy men and Moktee felt that if he could learn the art of negotiating with the customers that this would be something that he would like to do. The next day Moktee got another job with another vendor loading and unloading and helping the man sell his wares but it was not steady work. So he looked for something that would be steady work. Soon he found himself working in a cotton mill unloading and loading and keeping the machines running. It was a hard job from dawn to dust, it never changed. It was dusty, noisy, and dangerous.

He had heard that people could get hurt if they did not watch themselves around the machines. But it was steady work and soon by getting together with a couple of other young men, he could rent a room instead of sleeping in the streets. As bad as things had been before, Moktee now felt that things were actually getting better, if only a little bit. After a few months of working at the mill he was told by his overseer that a shipment of cotton that was supposed to have come in to keep the mill running was unexpectedly late and that there would be no work for the next couple of weeks until the ship arrived. So Moktee was out of work again. He went back to the market place but there was one day's work out of one week, two days in another week. The work here was not steady at all.

Every couple of days Moktee would check with the mill to find out if the ship would arrive on time so that he could get his mill job back but days stretched into weeks and Moktee thought that it would be a good idea for him to go down to the docks where the ships came in and to inquire about that ship or other ships that would be coming that maybe that would be a source of work for him.

So he eventually went down to the ship area and eventually found the shipping company that was supposed to bring the cotton and the ship that was so terribly late. They said that it was very common actually for the ships not to arrive on time and they did not think that it was a big deal.

They did not think it was important but of course to the workers like Moktee it was extremely important. So he decided that he would check down in the dock area every once in a while and maybe there would be other work there. While Moktee was at the harbor he came across many new sights, sounds, and smells. There were ships coming from faraway places all over the world. It was an education just to find out about these places. There were fishing boats, with local fishermen bringing great catches of fish. It was a remarkable place. One day there was a crowd of young men surrounding a British businessman who was promoting a strange and fantastic idea to the young men of Calcutta.

He said that there was plenty of work to be done across the ocean. More jobs than could be filled and that the shipping companies would bring the workers to these jobs in foreign countries for free. That all food would be given for the trip and when the workers arrive at the plantations on the faraway lands, they would be fed and housed and paid a small salary. Why, they could even save up the money and send some home if they liked. Of course, the only catch was you needed to sign up for five years. Moktee had never been out of his town before he came to the great city of Calcutta. He had been in Calcutta for less than a year. So the idea of signing up, although it was intriguing, was a little frightening because it would mean five years away from his country.

So Moktee thought about this a lot, and in his mind the good and the bad and what would be the possible opportunities. He had never before heard of a job where the employer had to feed you and house you and give you medical care. That was the most wonderful thing for the people of his town but unfortunately, they had to pack up and leave and go away for a long, long time. That was scary.

But the more Moktee thought of it, the more he began to realize that the work that he was able to get in Calcutta was not steady at all. The pay was very low. The conditions were harsh, he could not be sure of having a job from one day to another. The factories and employers would hire workers for a couple of weeks and then there would be no work at all. This was so very unstable, quite unsteady. He was captivated by the idea of having steady work and a steady house and steady food. How bad could it be in a far away country.

It was pretty bad where he was. Eventually he felt as though he had nothing to lose by signing up. It might be even a great adventure to go far, far away. He would save all his money. At the end of five years, he would come back with all his money saved up. That was his original idea when he came to Calcutta. Make extra money, save it up and go back to his town.

Why, maybe this indentured laborer system that the British businessman was talking about might just be the right thing for Moktee to sign up for. But this was certainly a very big step for a young man. He would have to think of this some more.

In another few days the ship would come in with the cotton, he could have his job back in the mill. He was a good worker. They liked him in the mill. Moktee thought about the overseas work but he went back to the mill and worked there several more months.

He thought and thought relentlessly what he would do. Finally he decided that he was going to do it. He said he had nothing to lose, it sounded like a good deal. I am still young and five years is not that long. I will come back with money in my pocket and maybe in five years conditions will be better in my home country and I would not have to worry about working or I can set up a small business.

So he made up his mind. In another couple of days there was no more work at the mill and he was again out of work. And so he decided to go down to the docks and sign up. So sign up he did. He had never signed a contract before. He did not even know what a contract was, but the British had an interpreter who read all the conditions of the contract so that he could understand exactly what he needed to do.

"Ah, he said I have signed up, what I am getting into I can't turn back, but I have no job here" and he waited for the next ship. He did not know where in the world he may be sent. The British system could send workers to any of the British colonies, and they were all over the world. Finally, everything was ready, he was assigned a ship one day, and two days later he would be leaving. The name of the ship was the *Equestrian* and it was headed for a place on the other side of the world. An island called "Trinidad".

He would be most likely assigned to work in a sugar plantation. He was ready to go. He was very optimistic. He was no longer afraid and he was looking forward to it. He was happy to go, he was determined that this would be a good thing for him. He would make the best of it and work hard, be a good worker, be admired, get promoted and come home with his money. Two days later he was gone.

Chapter 2

THE BRITISH IN INDIA

First Contact

The chief influence for the migration of Indians to various locations all over the world was the British Empire. The British Empire had a hand in several markets and locations throughout the world, including growing sugar cane, cotton, and making textiles. The great need to provide raw materials and labor for industries in Britain encouraged the policy of raising crops such as sugar cane and cotton in various parts of the British Empire, and if one area of the Empire had a shortage of labor, the population of India could always be relied upon to fill the need. The British encouraged the migration of vast numbers of Indian laborers, especially during the time of periodic famines that would always occur in India.

In places such as the Caribbean, slave labor had been used, but in 1834 Britain outlawed slavery throughout the Empire. Although slavery was brought to an end, plantations still required huge numbers of laborers. Slavery came to be replaced by a system of indentured contract laborers who were only slightly better off than slaves.

The India that the British took over was a very complex society, which had five or six major religions, at least ten different languages, and a history that stretched back to before the Greek and Roman empires. In 326 BC, India was invaded by Alexander the Great, and the first Moslem invasion was that of the Arabs in the seventh century AD. But these reached only a short distance into India. Much more successful was the invasion by Mohammed Ackbar, who overran much of the Ganges Plain area in the late twelfth century. The Moslem Sultanate was founded in 1206, and, by the end of the thirteenth century, the Moslem influence began to penetrate all the way to the south of India. Late in the fourteenth century came the incursion of Tamerlane, and, in the second decade of the sixteenth Century, Babur (a descendent of Genghis Khan) founded the Mogul Empire in northern India. Babur's grandson Ackbar became emperor in 1556. Ackbar was noted as one of the world's great rulers. Ackbar's grandson was the Emperor Shah Jahan, the builder of the beautiful Taj Mahal. This building bankrupted the country however, and in 1638 his son, Aurangzabe, deposed Shah Jahan and ruled for fifty years until he died in 1707.

When Europeans made contact with India in the sixteenth Century, The Mogul Empire was at its height in wealth and power. The British made their first contact with India when Elizabeth I was queen of England and Ackbar ruled all of India. In 1583, four English traders went to India. One of them returned to England in 1591 and told of the riches to be had. The British East India Company was formed in 1600, with the objective of going to the Spice Islands, but not necessarily to India. Their third voyage in 1607 had the secondary objective of trading with the West coast of India. The East India Company completed twelve voyages to India, and in 1613 the British were allowed to establish a trade center in the town of Surat on India's West coast. In 1639, the Englishman Francis Day established a small fort, which later became the town of Madras. In 1650, the Mogul Emperor allowed the British to establish a trading base on the east coast, which eventually became the city of Calcutta. In 1658, Madras became the headquarters of the East India Company. Bombay was ceded to the Portuguese in 1534, but in 1661 the title passed to Charles II of England. Seven years later the king transferred the city to the East India Company and by 1687 Bombay superseded Madras as the headquarters of the British East India Company.

By the early 1700's these three places in India were already beginning to bear a distinctive British stamp. The

Mogul Emperor Aurangzabe died in 1707, and the Empire slowly disintegrated after that. The Moguls had set up an elaborate administrative structure, most of which was simply taken over by the British. In a sense, the Moguls actually helped the British surpass them by being so well organized. Persians attacked Dehi in 1739 and carried off, among other things, the famous "Peacock Throne" used until recently by the rulers of Iran.

In June, 1756, the famous " black hole of Calcutta" incident occurred where rebels raided Calcutta and took 146 English men and confined them overnight in a jail 15 ft. by 18 ft. In the morning only 23 were still alive. Although there doesn't seem to be any particular cruelty intended by the Indians (other than crowding so many prisoners in such a small jail), the English became determined to avenge the black hole incident and regain their position of authority in Calcutta.

In 1765 The British East India Company became responsible for collecting taxes and making payments to the Moguls. This represented a major turning point in which the British began to collect taxes and administer justice. By not collecting taxes from their own citizens in their own country, the Mogul empire had ceded *de facto* control to the British. From 1798 onward, British involvement in India was based more on conflict with the French than with the Moguls. The British had to take steps to get rid of the French colonials and take over French parts of India. Prior to that, it was a pretty much unintentional British intrusion into India, mainly for trading. But after 1798, fighting became a more effective way of getting rid of the French, so much so that 1818 is normally given as the date when the British finally took complete control of all India. Indeed, after 1818, although there were Mogul emperors still around, they were on pension, and after 1818 there was no power left in all of India that could seriously challenge the British.

The story of the Indian takeover by the British is indeed an extraordinary one. England was a small island in the Atlantic, which, at the beginning of this story, was still fighting for its life against stronger countries in Europe. This tiny country had now come to rule the entire Indian sub-continent (with a population the size of all Europe) ten thousand miles away by sea, on the other side of the world. Even Englishmen never ceased to be amazed by this, and it is considered one of the strangest of all political anomalies. India remained a British colony until August 15th, 1947.

Chapter 3

RELIGIOUS AND CULTURAL DIVERSITY

Religious diversity and religious conflicts are inherent to the story of India, as well as with the various groups in India. The culture of India is diverse. Many different languages and religions somehow all are blended together. The list of the major cultures that make up the country of India are: Punjabi, Rajpur, Utah, Guparanci Maranthas, and Drividians consisting of Tamils, Wahras, Karandigas, Maharajahs, and the Parses.

The linguistic groups within India are: the Mauryans, Turks, Mughals, Afghans, Greeks, Persians, and Mongolians. There were also colonies of the British, French, Spanish, and Portuguese. There are a dozen principal languages in India and many minor languages that are still used.

There were different racial groups within India, too. The Caucasians, Austerloids, Mongolians, Dravidians, and the Huns. India was also the religious birthplace of Hinduism, Buddhism, Jainism, and Sikhism. Then Muslims arrived in the tenth century. When the French came they took Indians as slaves to their colonies. The English, Dutch, Spaniards, and Portuguese, in order to run their empires and colonies also took vast numbers of laborers from India and brought them to other parts of their colonies to work on the farms and plantations. But they were not taken as slaves but as indentured laborers. Some of the poor and destitute farming people of lower castes were anxious to go because of the desperate times in India, because of famines, lack of food or because of floods or loss of land. The indenture system allowed of a lot of people who volunteered and went away, to decide on their own never to ever come back.

India obtained its independence in 1947. Pakistan also obtained its independence in 1947; then Bangladesh split from Pakistan in 1971. Altogether the Indian subcontinent, consisting of India, Bangladesh, Pakistan, Nepal, Bhutan, and Sri Lanka (Ceylon) total over a billion people.

A notable thing about the political scene in India is that there is no "Uncle Sam" or "John Bull" character that symbolizes the country called India. In the US, Uncle Sam represents the whole country. All the people of the country together are "Uncle Sam," and the same is true in England with "John Bull." But there is no equivalent person, mythical figure, or even cartoon character that represents all of India. The reason is that India is much too diverse for that. There is no national unity symbol or identity figure. India is a land of contradictions-there is poverty alongside luxury; there is the gentle and the cruel, and splendor amid the mud huts. There's the Ponti, the people with plenty to eat, and the Outcasts, the people with just a handful of rice- just enough to get them through the day.

There are the meat-eaters and the vegetarians. There are those with force and power, those with deep thoughts and non-violence. And people who believe in veneration and respect for cows and other animals all living side by side. There are people, even in modern times, that do hand-spinning and weaving. There are businessmen who will interrupt a business meeting to go into meditation, businessmen who make business deals only after consulting an astrologer. None of this is thought of as unusual in the mixture and diversity that is India today.

In the West, the universe is thought of as real, solid and unmovable. But to many Indian religions, the solid earth and everything we see is merely an illusion. Reality, to them, exists on a higher plane than our Earthly world.

Chapter 4

INDIAN EMIGRATION TO OTHER COUNTRIES

In the period from 1896 to 1902, in the first great wave to leave India, 40,000 workers left to build the railway in East Africa. They went to Kenya, Uganda, and Tanzania. There was also much emigration of Indians to many other parts of the world. So much so, that by 1911 the US and Canada had put a halt all Indian Immigration. In 1914 a boatload of Indian laborers was actually stopped in the harbor of Vancouver in British Columbia and returned to India without anyone being allowed to leave the ship.

With the split of India from Britain in 1947, it turned out that many of the Hindu Indians who came from the Moslem area now called Pakistan, decided to migrate to Britain if they could; with the religious controversy these people were basically displaced from their own land. The Hindus who lived in Muslim Pakistan had no place to go. They could move to India to be with other Hindus, but would not have family there, or a place to live. The same was true in reverse with Muslims who lived in the mostly Hindu Indian section and wanted to go to Pakistan. As a result, many of them hoped to go to Britain, too. As the work in East Africa shut down, many Indians living abroad also went to Britain. Then in 1962 all Indians were expelled from Burma, which had been a large British colony. Burma had taken in many Indians, but when the British left, due to racial and religious tensions, thousands of Indians were ordered out of Burma. Many of these families had been in Burma for several generations, and now had no roots in India at all. In 1972 Uganda ordered all Asians out of the country. Most of these Asians who left went to England also.

Most of the laborers who left were Hindus from Northern India. They left to go to the various countries with the indentureship laws. Approximately two-thirds of the Indians who left India decided to remain in their adopted countries after they had fulfilled their contracts. It is not that they didn't like India, but they stayed chiefly because in their present condition, even with as little as they earned were better off than they would have been back in India.

As a result of indentureship, Indians moved to North and South America, the West Indies, and the British Colony of Mauritius. Five thousand went to Guyana;

240,000 to Trinidad; 144, 000 to Natal in South Africa; 50,000 to Fiji; 61,000 to Burma, Malaysia, and Singapore. At the end of their contracts,

Indian immigrants became free laborers within these foreign lands. They could leave the estate in search of employment in the towns. As free laborers, within these foreign lands, they were in great demand as workers on the estates, and many stayed. Indentured laborers and free laborers received the same rate of pay. On the plantation there were also opportunities for advancement: there were managers, overseers and foremen. Many of the Indian workers became foremen. Eventually however, the policy of indentured labor officially ended in 1917.

In the period between 1963 and 1965, the US, Canada, and Australia passed laws outlawing race as a factor in determining who could enter the country. Race alone could no longer be used to disqualify someone for admittance into the country, as it had been before. The new laws stressed educational qualifications. For the most part these countries said that they would admit anyone of any race as long as they had the job skills and education that would be useful to the country. This meant that fewer laborers were admitted, and more engineers, doctors and other highly skilled people came instead.

Chapter 5

INDIAN IMMIGRATION TO TRINIDAD

In Trinidad, East Indian immigration began on May 30, 1845 with the arrival of the first East Indian immigration ship *The Rozack* from Calcutta. There were 197 men, one infant and 28 women. In all, 240,000 laborers eventually came from India to Trinidad. Almost all came from Madras or Calcutta. What impelled the Indians to leave their homes and sign up as indentured laborers overseas? A survey was taken of the few men and women who had actually been born in India and by the various Trinidad-born who had asked their own parents and grandparents. Surprisingly, most Indians claimed to be have been tricked by the recruiting agents who played upon their youth and ignorance with stories of high wages and easy work sifting sugar in Trinidad. Some came for the adventure, a few came escaping the law, and a few because of family conflicts. But most came because food, money, and employment were non-existent at home. One old man from the village said that the recruiting agents had promised him all sort of things but *he* didn't believe them; so he wasn't surprised at all when they failed to materialize. He came expecting to work hard all his life for a little bit of pay. Nevertheless, he was not sorry he had come because he suspected that in India he would have fared much worse.

Most of these people however, said that they spent their first years in Trinidad crying and remembering their homes, realizing how badly they had been tricked. Many of the sons and daughters of those first Indians were almost unanimous in their belief that their fathers, their grandfathers and their grandmothers were "damn fools" for allowing themselves to be tricked. Whatever the truth, many of the Indians of Trinidad are convinced that their presence in the West Indies today is due to trickery, and, as they see it, the plantations, the recruiting agents, and the colonial government at the time were all parties to this deception.

It is very important to know, however, that whether the recruiting agents were guilty of fraud, misrepresentation, or trickery, conditions in India at the time of the greatest indentured immigration were such that the only choice for many of these people was to leave India as an indentured laborer or stay in India and suffer a slow but almost certain death from starvation.

Whatever the truth is, it is clear that most remained in Trinidad although all contracts provided for a free return trip to India. The idea that some of the members of the Indian population were tricked into indenture persists to this day. But this is difficult to prove or disprove. The record indicates that the system of indentured immigration was not without its abuses. Although there was a "Protector of Emmigrants" as an official post in the port of Calcutta, his legal power to prevent injustices and abuses was very limited.

It is known that immigration agents of the British Colonies appointed professional recruiters who were generally very unprincipled men. They frequented the Indian villages where crops had failed and also the pilgrim centers where thousands of illiterate and extremely poor people congregated. Here the good as well as the not-so-good recruiters cast their net. The recruiters received a commission of about three pounds sterling for every male and a little bit more for every female. For the recruiters the temptation was thus strong enough to inspire them sometimes to use means that were horribly cruel and totally dishonest. On the other hand, official documents of the day show that even if the right of a return passage was removed from the contract, it did not cut down on the number of laborers who would sign up for indenture. Bad harvests and a scarcity of food, which existed for so much of the time anyway, guaranteed that plenty of laborers would sign up. Experienced agents and recruiters knew how to take advantage of this situation. Famine, hunger, and want would overcome any hesitation that the laborers might have had. The agents could also play on the workers ignorance of the conditions and distances involved to get to the plantations. In addition, a quota requiring that a certain proportion of women be included among the immigrants only added to the abuses.

Because very few married men cared to come at all, most recruits were single men. But in India, among the Coolie (unskilled laborer) population, there is no class for respectable single women. To meet the female quota, the kidnapping of women and the recruitment of prostitutes and beggars was common. Medical examinations for all laborers were supposed to be made upon the signing of the contracts and before any journey, but the lack of any significant number of immigrants being rejected made one feel that the examinations may not have been adequate. Not only were pre-voyage examinations entirely unsatisfactory, but also an examination in the colonies upon arrival might cause the immigrants to be sent back as unfit, or in the event that they was permitted to remain, require them to labor at reduced wages.

Those few men still alive in the plantation villages of Trinidad who had actually gone through the examination gave another indication of the frivolous nature of the medical examinations. According to them, most potential recruits believed that only men in their twenties would be accepted. As a result they claimed that it was common for a boy of fourteen and a man of forty-five to both claim they were twenty-five years old, and for both to pass. Conditions at the arrival depots also were not good. The mortality rate was high, and desertion came to almost 5 percent.

Conditions on the ships bringing the laborers were appalling. Moreover, it is true that very few, if any, of the laborers had any more than a vague idea of the nature of the work involved. The wages were the minimal rate, equivalent to about twenty five cents per day. In the contract statement, their rations, their dwellings, their medical care etc. were given only in vague terms. But even when they were specific, they did not promise very much. There were some legal provisions, however, in each colony to prevent abuses in the allotment of laborers to the various estates. For instance, care was taken that children under the age of fifteen were not separated from their parents or guardians, and that relatives should be allowed to accompany each other and that even friends should not be separated unless unavoidable. But in spite of all of this, the laborers had "nothing to say in the matter of their allotment" and did not get to see their masters until they were put on the estate.

The coolies soon discovered that they had almost nothing to say about anything. The plantation owners could and did violate contracts with impunity, and the laborers were subject to sanctions about which they had not even been informed before leaving India. Despite all the contracts and ordinances, the rations, living and working conditions, medical care, and payment of wages were completely at the mercy at the plantation owners, and were quite often inferior to those the laborer had expected when he signed up. Even with the abuses one missionary worker wrote, "The condition of the coolies is comfortable and their treatment by the estate authorities is all that could be desired." However true this may have been in some instances, it is important to observe that it was entirely up to the estate managers to determine the nature of the working conditions. After all that has been said, the truth is that there is plenty of evidence that these conditions led to a higher than normal rate of suicide, sickness, despondency, and death among the coolies.

Upon his introduction to a plantation, the newly arrived laborer underwent a period of transition. Those who were weak or sickly suffered from the change but the strong and those with a desire to work soon become acclimated and worked readily. Whatever their various expectations or previous experience, almost all received the same assignment- they were put to work in the fields and mills. Work during crop time was long and arduous. It involved hard work in the fields and equally hard work in the mill buildings, loading trucks and manufacturing sugar- with women working alongside the men for 12, 14, and 16 hours at a stretch. Fieldwork involved forking, weeding, cutting cane and all the operations connected with the preparation and cultivation of the ground as well as and the harvesting of the crops.

The following is taken from a diary written in 1831 describing the general routine on a typical Trinidad estate: "Every weekday, overseers and drivers go around the barracks and the coolies are called and assigned their tasks and whoever is ill sent to the hospital. The laborers go to their tasks which are measured for them by their drivers and if they have any complaints to make when the manager rides around at 7 o'clock at which time he sees that fair assignments are given. The overseer has several gangs under him for plowing, fertilizing, and collecting fodder, all of which he visits in turn. Cooking for the day is generally done early every morning, about 4 a.m. A woman, who is paid ten cents per day, looks after babies and small children while the parents are in the fields. The manager said that in this estate he has never known a driver to strike a coolie. Neither do overseers ill-treat them. But during harvest time they have to be a little stricter, to get the work done in time".

The organization of the estate is described as follows: The sugar estates are owned by resident proprietors or by absentees. Local agents represent the absentees. The agents hire an estate manager who in turn is a person with whom the coolie has to deal directly. In one or two instances on the larger estates, the manager may have a deputy manager. But generally the next person to a manager is an overseer and the overseer directly superintends certain gangs in fields and in building work. The overseer is up early on his horse going through his portion of his estate and through the day overlooks the weeding, planting, and digging and takes an account in his field books of the people at work, noting whether they are in the fields or absent and the amount of money each earn in a day. In the evening, the overseer checks the hospital books to see if any of his workers have any sickness and were absent from work. His book then represents a record of the day's labor, which, after examination and certification by the manager, is transferred to the pay list. This document is then evidence of wages due to the worker, as well as proof, if necessary, in the magistrate's court of his absence or presence.

On any particular day, six or eight overseers may be found on a typical estate. Underneath the overseers are the foremen, frequently called drivers, who are the immediate supervisors of each gang. They watch the work, note the quality, and keep the laborers productive. Also on staff are an engineer, some sub-engineers, a bookkeeper, hospital staff, and a cook.

The number of laborers on a single estate varies from one or two hundred to a thousand. Available forces will be collected in gangs for various objects of work. The strongest will form the shuttle or cane-cutting gang at crop time. The less able will be the weeding and building gangs, and these will be subdivided into creole gangs, coolie gangs, and light work gangs of weaker men, women, and children who will be working at less demanding jobs. In the buildings will be found ninety to a hundred people at work; the rest are distributed all over the fields or in the hospital.

With only small modifications, such as an increase in bookkeeping staff, this table of organization on the estate is still in effect today, especially in Trinidad. It reflects very little change of organization from that which existed during the days of slavery. Then, the labor force consisted of Negro slaves. The incoming East Indian indentured laborers simply replaced the slaves in the plantation system. The wages, hours, and working conditions promised to the workers in India varied slightly from colony to colony but whatever the agreement, it had little binding force at all on the plantation or estate owner. For example, the immigrant signing up for Trinidad was told that he would be given a choice of working either nine hours a day for twenty cents a day or being paid by the task. That is, a specific amount of work for a fixed rate. Usually, nine-tenths of the work done on the estate was done by task. While the employer agreed upon task labor, it also benefited the worker, for he assumed that he might be able to finish the original task in less than nine hours or that by working harder he might be able to earn more money. Nevertheless, a major effect of the task system was to put the laborer completely at the mercy his superiors. These superiors determined the nature of the work to be done and decided whether or not it had been completed in a satisfactory manner. The laborer's right to protest a superior's decision was negligible.

In fact, in some estates if the overseer was dissatisfied with the work, as a punishment to the laborer, his workbook could be left blank for the day or a cross entered instead of a price, which means that the laborer would get nothing for that day. Living quarters provided for the indentured laborers were either those vacated by the freed slaves or similar new buildings. In addition to the crowded and unhealthy conditions, the laborers had little right to privacy. For example, even though they were indentured laborers, not slaves, it was common practice for employers to open the doors of workers' houses in the morning to turn them out to work. Another big problem was that of not recruiting enough women to fill the quota. From 1877 to 1878, a total of 18,488 immigrants came from Calcutta, but only 6,000 (or less than a third) were females. The shortage of women was a source of much conflict between the men. Many plantation managers complained about the small proportion of women, and no doubt, the lack of women caused problems for the management as there were many jealousies and quarrels. A good-looking woman received much admiration, but it was impossible for every man to have a wife of his own, even if he wished to have one. This situation created a breeding ground for prostitution. The lack of privacy in the quarters, the presence of prostitutes, and the general shortage of women, all appeared to have led to strain and conflict. It is clear that conflicts and crimes growing out of the absence of women among the indentured laborers would lead to the fact that even marriage among the coolies would be in a state of chaos. The plantation system had developed during slavery and it did not substantially change during the period of indentured labor. No provision was made for behavior patterns appropriate to the immigrants' origin or customs. By the very nature of the system there was very little opportunity for them to follow their customs and habits. Women were scarce, and raising a traditional family was almost impossible. Even where a family existed, plantation conditions conflicted with normal Indian family life, as may be seen from the high rate of conflict and crime growing out of Indian male-female relationships on the plantations.

Even though living and working conditions of the indentured laborers was similar to the previous Negro slave conditions, there was one important difference. Slavery was for life, while indentured labor, in principle at least, was for a fixed period of time-usually five years. The slaves knew that there was no possibility of return, but the indentured laborer could dream of going home some day or otherwise living again according to the patterns of his culture.

The number of years for which an Indian contracted to serve as an indentured laborer varied only slightly from colony to colony throughout the nineteenth century. In many cases, another five years of residence, but as a free laborer was required. Free return passage was usually available but not always provided for in the contract. The first laborers had no intention of staying once their period of indenture was over. They saved as much of their pay as they could and were determined to return home. Furthermore, this attitude on their part was initially supported and approved by the plantation owners and Colonial authorities because it aided recruiting of new workers.

After a few years however, the needs of the plantation owners changed and conflicted with the needs of the laborers. The plantation owners wanted to maintain a continuous supply of cheap labor. They now objected to the cost of providing return passage, as well as to the cost of recruiting replacements. They objected to returns as they now considered it the draining of part of their "wealth"- (the laborers themselves) - from the colonies back to India. But the strong desire of the laborers to return home persisted. Various attempts were made by the plantation owners to deal with this situation. In fact, in the island of Mauritius, plantation owners withdrew the promise of a free return passage. Not surprisingly, this led to a falling off in the numbers willing to immigrate to the colony. Some colonies such as Guadeloupe passed laws intended to keep all its Indian laborers in a perpetual state of servitude. Conditions for return passage were made so difficult that the laborer was left with no real alternative other than to sign up again. Some laborers were in their fourth, fifth, and even sixth indenture terms. Another approach to this problem was to entice the laborer to stay of his own free will after the completion of his contract. In British Guiana, East Indians were offered special privileges if they would remain on the estates as free laborers. In Trinidad it was possible for East Indians to actually purchase small plots of land. This was unique. It was not only attractive to the laborer newly released out of his indenture, but it made possible the formation of Indian villages and contributed to the retention of Indian culture in Trinidad more than in the other colonies. Owning his own land would have been out of the question back in India, where only the rich owned land.

This approach served to the advantage of the Trinidad planters and the workers also. Because of the long "slack" season in Trinidad, many estates preferred to have a ready source of non-indentured labor. These East Indians could usually earn only a bare subsistence living from their own plots of land and therefore were eager to work on the estates during crop planting and harvest time. The estates were spared the expense, in turn, of providing for them during the non-crop season.

Despite all inducements, Indians continued to return home after completing their indentures. However, many did stay on, and a sizable proportion of those remained in the rural areas. In Trinidad, many free Indians settled down on government land or vacant land, forming villages comparatively isolated from land owned by the British Crown or the plantations. In these villages the Indians established themselves much the same way as they had been in India. They built the same type of houses, wore the same clothes, spoke the same language, and worshipped the same gods in the same kinds of temples.

But for how long could the Indian villages in Trinidad remain the same as they were in India? Even though these villagers were Indians, they and their children were Trinidadians as well. The East Indian villages were within a larger Trinidad country, which affected the lives of all the villagers. Nonetheless, it is clear that in Trinidad some cultural traditions of India persisted. Considering the obstacles, it would not be surprising had the East Indians merged completely into Trinidad culture, maintaining few if any of their cultures and rituals. This is in fact what did happen in British Guiana and some of the other colonies. The important thing is that the unique custom in Trinidad of granting laborers who had finished their indenture period the right to buy small plots of land and form little villages, contributed immensely to the keeping of Indian culture and religion, customs, and clothing alive in Trinidad more than in the other colonies. This has persisted even until today. In spite of that, there would be social problems in integrating thousands of laborers who came into the colonies without a family. Most Indians came to Trinidad as individuals or perhaps with one or two friends at a time. They did not come as families or social groups, religious groups, or other groups. Neither did they have many of the things that would help to bind them together. They were just a group of individuals, signing up for work, and then, at the end of their term, trying to recreate an Indian society which they could only remember as individuals.

Indian indentured laborers did not emigrate in kinship groups or village groups, and rarely even in small family groups. They left their original culture system and went to Trinidad, British Guiana, and other territories containing what was for them an alien social structure. The individual had little place in the new social structure, which was based on work gangs. When these individuals tried to re-create their home community, after they had served their indentures, there was little in common to build upon.

The East Indian immigrants who came together in the late 1880s to try to form the nucleus of a village faced great problems trying to reconstruct anything like their previous Indian village life. Generally speaking, they were strangers to each other; although they shared a common culture, it was derived from different villages in Northern India. They were not kinsmen, extended families or even village neighbors; they were strangers to one another who shared some common memories and similar but different communities. For them to form a community, some consensus had to be achieved as to what constituted appropriate behavior for all the necessary relationships and institutions. Common agreement could not easily be reached, and it was likely to be more difficult in the case of some institutions than in others. The distribution of the caste system is just one example of an important cultural institution presenting its own special obstacles to any attempt at reconstruction of village life.

Apart from their own internal difficulties, immigrants to Trinidad faced serious external problems, too. The nature of labor on the sugar plantations operated to weaken important elements of East Indian social structure. When everyone is a plantation laborer, there are no familiar caste structures. Other Indian customs and religious practices were restricted and sometimes even forbidden. For example, Hindu cremation was not possible, and Hindu marriages actually had no legal standing until 1946. Thus, the rebuilding of Indian village social structure had to take place, but within the context of Trinidad society. The people who lived in these independent villages depended upon the larger Trinidad plantations for their cash income, and their descendants are similarly dependent today. Relations with non-Indians were important to them then and are important now. Finally, it is clear that whatever the obstacles were, in Trinidad, more than in many other places, the hardships were overcome, social structures were put back together, and some parts of a loose fabric of an Indian community was woven back into place, enough to keep the cultural lines growing strong right up until the present day.

Back in India, however, the indentured system came under fire for some of the crooked and unsavory methods of recruitment and the constant problem of never being able to find enough female recruits. Indeed, during January and February of 1917, Mahatma Gandhi made emigration the centerpiece of his first big political campaign in India, and he spoke against indenture repeatedly. So much so, that the year 1917 brought the end of the indenture system. East Indians, whose term of indenture had expired, automatically joined the rest of the island's free labor workforce. Having been relieved from the restriction of indenture, the new status of free labor afforded workers a choice of occupations. Despite this, the majority stuck to employment on the land, and they took jobs in agriculture and farming. Free Indians worked in regular gangs on the estates doing much of the same work they had performed during their indenture service. Most of the workers were housed on the estates, and some were given plots of land where sugar cane could be raised and sold to their employers. This scheme became popular enough to attract 6,000 Indian cane farmers by 1912. As more indentured laborers assumed the status of free men, the supply of free Indian laborers grew, and many of the estates employed free laborers only.

Some Indians also made a living as owners of carts and carriages; the initial cost of which was money they had managed to save or borrow. Carts were owned by the drivers or their relatives. Indians were also employed as police constables at a starting salary of forty-five pounds sterling rising to a maximum of seventy five pounds per year. Lower on the scale were laborers employed in the southern parts of the island by the public works department; the majority of these men earned the equivalent of between thirty to fifty cents per day.

Another steady source of employment was the clearing of forest and planting of cocoa by contract. Work in these areas lasted for a period of five years during which a cash payment of 25 cents per tree was made to laborers. Through regular employment of this kind, some laborers, despite their meager earnings, accumulated enough money to buy their own land. Many Indians worked for private employers as gardeners, grooms, porters, and watchmen. Some, after many years of saving, became shopkeepers, traders, and landowners, thus becoming employers themselves. By 1912 the total area of land owned by Indians amounted to 89,000 acres. Plantation owners, in lieu of return passages to India, made grants of land. Consequently, many Indians gradually evolved into a land-owning class. With the end of indenture, East Indian immigration was severely reduced. Consequently, many Indians after their term had expired, refused to work in the sugar cane estates. They now said that their intention was to buy a cow, then a shop. The principal employment for Indians was as hotel keepers, peddlers, and small merchants about town. When at long last their term of Indentureship had ended, the Indians gradually evolved into a merchant class or bought land and became farmers or agricultural contractors.

Chapter 6

THE ISLANDS OF TRINIDAD AND TOBAGO

On his third voyage in 1498, Christopher Columbus discovered Trinidad and claimed it for Spain. The native Carib and Arawak Indians were enslaved by the Spaniards but by the late 1700s, the Spaniards mostly ignored Trinidad, as other ventures seemed more profitable. The British later conquered the Spanish settlements, and later both islands fought for their Independence, which they attained in 1797. The British left behind their sport called cricket, which the people grew fond of, and today it is the national sport of Trinidad. Trinidad is rich in oil and does not advertise for tourists as much as the other Caribbean islands, but still it has become a serious tourist destination. People come not only for the variety of beaches but also to visit one of the biggest bird sanctuaries in the world.

Port of Spain, like so many cities with bustling shopping centers, fast food stands, modern hotels, and active night life, draws mixed reviews. The countryside is calmer. Trinidad, with so many different races, is a melting pot; the main religions are Christianity, Hinduism, and Islam. All these religions are practiced and do not cause conflict but rather work very well together.

Tobago, Trinidad's sister island, is about twenty miles from Trinidad and it is connected by air-lines and ferries. The physical beauty of the island is absolutely stunning, especially the forests of fruits, cocoa, and citrus. Tobago, surrounded by tropical beauty and lush landscapes with a spectacular reef, is a great escape from the big city. Those who like white sand, sun, and solitude in a mellow atmosphere will enjoy this type of Tobago. Scarborough, the capital of Tobago, is calm and plain but the local market is something to see-with a wide variety of colorful fruits and vegetables that you can't find anywhere else but in this little island. Most of the shops are clustered in streets around the market. Shoppers find the echo of the vendors exciting with their wares being offered quite similar to an auction. Tourists especially like this kind of bargaining because the vendors eventually do not want their items to remain unsold at the end of the day, so the shoppers take advantage of this chance to bargain.

Trinidad and Tobago, an oil rich nation, is nearer to South America than any of the other commonwealth Caribbean island countries. It is because of the production of oil, steel, and petrochemicals that Trinidad has the largest income among the other Commonwealth Caribbean island countries. Trinidad is in the West Indies. It lies in the Caribbean Sea near the north-east coast of South America. Trinidad is near Venezuela (7 miles to the southwest) and the smaller island, Tobago is about twenty miles north-east of Trinidad. Trinidad and Tobago is a Republic. The Prime Minister, who is usually the leader of the majority party in Parliament, serves as the head of the government. Most of the people are of African or Indian descent. Other groups of Chinese and Europeans form the rest of the population. English is the country's official language. Spanish and Hindi are also spoken, and many people speak Trinidadian English, a form of English with French and Spanish influences. Roman Catholics form the largest religious group, followed by Hindus and Anglicans. Tropical forests and fertile plants cover much of Trinidad. The mountain range extends east and west across the northern area and hills rise in the central and southern section.

Trinidad and Tobago has a hot and humid climate, indeed. The economy of Trinidad and Tobago is based mainly on oil production. Sixty million barrels of oil are produced annually in Trinidad and it imports additional oil for refining. Petroleum and minerals account for about eighty percent of the country's export income. On the other hand, Pitch Lake in Trinidad is the world's chief source of natural asphalt, a tar-like substance that is used for paving roads. Sugar, the chief export crop, is also used to produce molasses and rum.

Trinidad and Tobago has about 4,000 miles of roads and an airport on each island. The country has two daily newspapers, a TV station, and two major radio stations. The Spanish set up a permanent settlement on the island in 1592, but the population did not begin to grow rapidly until 1783. A land grant offer was made by Spain in that same year, and Roman Catholic settlers came to the island to develop the economy. They established sugar plantations and the island prospered. But the British captured Trinidad in 1797 and took possession of the island for the next 150 years. Though the Spanish settlers fought for possession, Britain took control of Trinidad. Although thousands of black slaves had been brought from Africa to work on the island's plantations, labor shortages occurred after Britain abolished slavery in 1833.

Many African workers did not stay on the plantations, so workers were brought from India to work in the cane fields. During the great depression of the 1930s, the colony suffered severe economic setbacks. The people then demanded a greater voice in their government, and Britain allowed a gradual increase in self-government during the 1940s and 1950s. The colony became an independent nation in 1962.

Through the years, immigrants from every corner of the world-from Africa, the Middle East, Europe, India, China, and the Americas-have visited and stayed in the country. It is against this background that the island has become the fascinating mixture of races and creeds that it is today. Trinidad, (which is the size of Delaware) and Tobago together form the nation popularly known as T& T. South African Bishop Desmond Tutu once called it "The Rainbow Country" for its abundance of floral growth and the diversity of its population. The islands are the most southern outposts of the West Indies. Trinidad lies only seven miles from Venezuela, to which it was physically connected in prehistoric times. The Spanish founded Trinidad in 1592 and held it longer than any other real estate. The English settled Tobago in 1642, and they captured Trinidad in 1797. Both islands remained in British hands until the two island nations declared independence in 1962.

Culture of the Twins Islands

Carnival Parade

Trinidad, known as the land of the humming bird, is the birthplace of calypso, steel drum music, the limbo, and is known for its beautiful beaches. Trinidad used to be visited only by business travelers going to Port of Spain. They were not interested in tourism, but rather in resources such as sugar, oil, natural gas, and steel. Trinidad is one of the most industrialized nations in the Caribbean, and it exports oil and asphalt to the western hemisphere. It is also the home of Angostura bitters used mostly for cocktails. This recipe is a guarded secret, much the same as the formula for Coca Cola.

Carnival *is* Trinidad and Tobago. It is the land where the steel band, calypso, and the limbo were born. Year-round, the sound of the big metal drums can be heard in towns and in the hills. Women take part in this festival as well. Carnival is a parade, in which thousands of people form bands, thronging through the choked streets, from early morning until midnight, for two solid days. Calypso singers poke fun at individuals, criticize the government, and laugh at serious situations. Their themes can be intellectual, funny, constructive, and, sometimes even destructive. In the weeks before Carnival, tents are put up, and the calypsonians, under the auspices of a group or organization, offer nightly previews to the public of their versatility and skill.

A Carnival masque band is a group of masqueraders. They number up to several hundred bands, vying for the title of "best band." In their entire splendor the bands create a dazzling panorama of moving color, pulsating their way through the streets, marching and dancing to the music, up to the grandstand. The winning band is given a prize of a couple of thousand of dollars. The costumes that are created for Carnival are true works of inventive art. Most of the costumes are magnificently and carefully decorated with light-reflecting tinsel or sprayed surfaces. With research and design, it takes about a year to come into full production of this great event. There is a great contest and victory is declared when the best band is chosen and given the prize. From the time I was a little child my dad would gather the family together and a few friends from the neighborhood and go to the Carnival. We were all packed like sardines in his van and very eager to see the wonderful parade and costumes.

I can still remember how glad I was to see this special event. Our servant came with us and prepared delicious sandwiches such as shark fish and bread and also pilaf together with tropical fruit drinks. There was enough food to last the entire day. In Port of Spain the main city, my dad found a parking spot for the day. I remember him saying "do not leave the van, just stay in your seats and watch the bands as they go by." Of course, sitting in the van we had very good seats to watch everything that was going on. He was particularly concerned about all the noise, confusion and the crowds walking around and feared that one of us might get lost. I was awed and looked all around at everything that was happening. My father bought us ice cream cones and the cones, because of the heat dripped over my hands, dripped over my clothes as I was watching the bands. The music thrilled me. I even got up and danced. We stayed there all day and around sunset we were tired and headed back home. I only wished that I was old enough to be in one of those parades and someday I thought that I would be in the band itself. I loved the carnival because there was nothing like it. It was just fun. My dad wanted to give his kids a good time and everybody regardless of race or religion would be sure to turn out once a year for this magnificent celebration.

Beaches of Trinidad and Tobago

The months from June to August are the best time to go to the beaches. Life guards are on the beach daily in case of accidents, and red flags indicate unsafe bathing areas. One of the most popular spots is Maracas Beach which is about forty five minutes from Port of Spain. It has beautiful white sand, and it is ideal for surfing because of the high waves. Facilities are well maintained, with a large parking lot, tables with benches, and rooms with showers, toilets and lockers. Visitors enjoy a variety of tasty food from the local vendors; especially bake (biscuit) and shark. On the hill, there is a restaurant and bar from which the visitors can enjoy the scenery and tranquility. Tours are also provided within the area.

Mayaro Beach

Another beach, Mayaro Bay, located on the East Coast, is the longest on the island. It is about a two hour drive from Port of Spain. Along the beach, there are a number of guesthouses and small hotels and several properties for rent near the more popular bathing areas.

Las Cuevas Beach

There are other beaches found on the island. This beach, unlike Maracas and Mayaro, is more sheltered and even though it is some distance to reach people find it attractive. The clarity of the water and the calm waves are excellent for swimming, making one not want to get out of the water. Service amenities are included and this beach is less than an hour's drive from Port of Spain.

Pigeon Point

Pigeon Point, on the leeward side of Tobago, is the island's best beach, covered with miles and miles of beautiful sand. Swimming is ideal in these calm waters, and visitors go over to the famous and magnificent Bucco Reef to swim and see the wonderful corals and fish that live in the ocean. I still remember my father taking the family there. I was afraid at first to go diving but eventually did, as the rest of my brothers and sisters took their first steps. I remember being filled with excitement.

Bird Watching in Tobago

The famous bird sanctuary draws attention from people coming far and wide to see all types of birds living in harmony, and it is a must for visitors to see. Most of the human population of the island is concentrated on the southern end of Tobago. The rest of the people live in villages strung out along the coastline. In fact, sixty percent of the island is not developed. The larger estates are abandoned or taken over by real estate developers, so at least in the short term there is an increase of wildlife. Tobago may not have as many animals as its neighbor, Trinidad, but it is a great bird watching area. In a few days, bird watchers can investigate the sanctuary of birds of all different species and colors. The village of Seaside, north along the coast, is the only place one can see the humming birds, brown boobies, white-tipped doves, flycatchers, and all other species in the wetlands. Bird watching tours are easily arranged because of the knowledgeable guides; the journey by minibus develops into one of the highlights of the tour. The Mangrove

Swamps are situated south of Pigeon Point and Bucco Marsh. Large iguanas are sometimes seen in the crowns of the mangroves. These funny creatures splash into the water at the least bit of noise. Surprisingly, the mangroves are noisy with moorhens and other similar species creating pandemonium throughout the undergrowth. The Bucco Marsh accommodates shorebirds and waders, black-bellied and whistling ducks, but the scarlet ibis birds refuse to make the marsh a permanent home because of all the noise.

Chapter 7

MY HISTORY

The Contract

This is the story of those West Indians who, like so many other US immigrants, left their homeland to seek a better life. In the beginning my ancestors came from north central India, from a small and very poor state called Bihar.

My great, great grandfather, Mohammed Moktee, worked for five years as an indentured laborer. Indentured laborers started to come to Trinidad around 1844, and the system was finally ended in 1917. Obtaining cheap labor was so important that the Trinidad Government used tax money to pay a third of the cost of transporting the workers from India to Trinidad, and after their term of service was over, the government would pay part of the transportation home.

Because government tax money was involved, the government stepped in to set the wages for the new immigrants. Under the British system, of course, they kept very careful records. According to these records, every able-bodied worker who worked one day was paid one shilling, one and one and a half pence. That is equal to about 25 cents per day or about $6.00 per month. As previously mentioned, if a worker was legitimately unable to work for some reason he would still receive his ordinary wages for the day. This was not a free ride however, and if the worker was not otherwise productive, his indenture could be canceled and he could be returned to India.

Most of the plantations in Trinidad raised cocoa or sugar, and most of the indentured laborers from India found themselves working on the sugar estates. The work was mostly hoeing, forking, and weeding of the sugar cane. There were also some skilled jobs for grooms, storekeepers, blacksmiths, carpenters, and watchmen who were paid wages higher than the ordinary laborer by as much as 50 to 100percent. The workday generally consisted of up to nine hours each day, except Sundays and holidays. But no worker was compelled to work more than forty five hours per week.

The day began at 6:00 to 6:30 in the morning and finished at 4:00 in the afternoon with a one hour break for lunch. The work year consisted of 260 days (equal to five days a week for 52 weeks). The work was hard for the new arrivals. Although most were farm workers from India, they were not used to the rigorous schedule of seven to nine hours a day, five to five and a half days a week, imposed by the plantations. They were used to long hours of casual work done at a slow pace. They all had to go through a couple of weeks of initiation or orientation to get used to the fast pace. Of course, the British system had its rules. All indentured laborers had to live on the plantation, and if a worker was found on a public highway or on land other than his employer's, he could be arrested and thrown in jail. But every indentured immigrant who had worked for two weeks was entitled to a leave of absence from the plantation for one day and one night. He was allowed no more than seven days leave at one time and no more than twenty six days in a year.

Around the year 1844 the British found themselves in a position where they had extensive mills in Britain for which they required large supplies of cotton and sugar for processing in their factories. Because of the shortage of these raw materials in England, they soon realized that in certain parts of the world they had colonies with the right climate and conditions to raise cotton and sugar cane. All they needed was a large army of laborers to work the fields and plantations in order to have a very successful farming industry. They came up with the idea of recruiting labor from India, which was overloaded with people, but with not enough resources to feed them. The

British would import them into the other colonies, where they needed large amounts of cheap labor to raise sugar cane or cotton. India was always overcrowded; always there were people without work. There was always thousands with not enough to eat, particularly in those times when there was famine, disease, floods, and a never-ending stream of bad things that could happen to the farming people that cultivated food for India. During the time of indentureship, famine and death became almost common every couple of years in northern India. The idea of the indentured labor contract seemed a very good one which allowed the poor, hungry, and starving excess laborers from India to go abroad and work in the Empire's farms and factories. This plan would help to produce the cotton, cloth, sugar, molasses, and rum that was needed in the other the colonies. This was a very workable plan for the British because they used excess labor from one colony to fill the labor shortages in other colonies. The indentured labor contract came about in 1844.

During the time of indentureship, they would recruit young men and women to be farm laborers and mill workers in other colonies, and these would be guaranteed, according to the British, that they were not slaves if they signed a contract. But what choice did these poor Indians really have? Either sign up, or stay there and starve. They were given a written contract. If they could not read it, somebody was assigned to read it to them, in their own language, explaining that they would be signing up for five years work in a foreign country.

Food would be provided for them during the journey, and food would be provided for them when they got there. The only thing that was required of them was a decent work ethic, which they would have to follow in India anyway. Then at the end of the five-year term they would be entitled to a return trip to India if they so desired. Or, if they wanted, they could sign up for another labor contract for another five years. Over the period of time that the indentured laborers were hired and transported to other colonies, the term of five years was extended first to seven years, then to ten years.

Brokers were pressured to extend the term of contract because the British increasingly needed more laborers in other parts of the world. The contract itself was a typically British kind of detail-oriented legalism detailing everything that was entitled to the worker. It does not seem to be too unfair given the labor conditions of the time. The workers were expected to work hard for what seems today like a small amount of money, but the truth is that was common-place in those days anyway. And the rewarding part of the contract was that if they signed up, they would actually be guaranteed food to eat every day, which was an amazing thing to them because that could not be guaranteed if they stayed home. Especially during the hard times, many of the Indian workers were happy to sign up to be indentured laborers to work for a period of time and to be given the option to come back after five or ten years, or to stay on if they grew accustomed to the plantations or the lands where they were sent: other Caribbean sites or to Trinidad.

The contract was legal, according to the British System. They would sign up and be legally bound to fulfill their part of the contract. Probably most did understand what was required of them and most went willingly, because staying home meant almost certain starvation and death. Many of them thought it was a lucky opportunity to have a contract where the people who hired you had to feed you every day. They certainly would not have that privilege by staying home in India. So although they were going on a long, long journey, - four months at sea to a far away land - to work very hard for small amounts of money, it was far better than staying where they were.

But when these people signed a piece of paper to go to a foreign land for work, they did not know all that lay before them. They knew there was famine and no work in their homeland. They did not expect gold, but just a bowl of rice to stop their hunger. In going to this strange land, they thought that they would have more than a few rupees and that wages and food would be given to them every day; at least they would not starve. If they stayed back, they would likely die of famine and disease. So they went aboard the ship by the hundreds to get away from the conditions in India. In their homeland, the cows, oxen, and goats were fed to produce crops and milk. They were sacred, but these Indians were poor, starving, and in search of better conditions, so they signed a contract that the British overseer read to them.

They thought perhaps that the journey was around the corner but had no idea it would take four months. Welfare payments or unemployment insurance did not exist in those times, and certainly in India there was no such system. The poor laborers made their choices based upon the British insistence that they would have a better life, and that after five years working in some kind of sugar plantation they would be released from their contracts and have enough money to do as they wanted. The contract then was both a blessing and a curse.

The Voyage of the *Equestrian*

The Departure

My great, great grandfather Mohammed Moktee was aboard the *Equestrian* when it sailed from Calcutta. The ship left for Trinidad on November 19, 1851. In the same ship may have been his future wife Modea, whom he did not meet aboard that vessel but later on. No record of Modea appeared among the passengers of this ship, or any other ship, as she was too young to be listed by name; she would have been simply listed as an infant. The voyage of the *Equestrian* was far more eventful than that of most other vessels. Most of these farm laborers had never seen an ocean before, much less travel upon one. If that wasn't frightening enough, rounding the Cape of Good Hope at the southern end of Africa brought turbulent waters, high waves, and pitch blackness. The Indians called it the "Mad Sea." Life at sea was panicky and disturbing for indentured laborers aboard the ship. First, there was a hurricane which dismasted the ship, and the effects of the raging hurricane suffocated some of the Indians to death.

Moktee was a survivor, and he saw the dilemma of the other passengers, their outrage at the ship's conditions. He braved himself through the hardship aboard the ship and vowed to make a success of himself when he landed. The Indians aboard clutched themselves and one another for comfort. Some lost their loved ones, and it was overbearing to hear the laborers scream and cry aboard the vessel. Moktee engaged himself by comforting others and gave a helping hand to the weaker passengers. All the Indians were troubled, unsatisfied, they cried out, "This is hell. I have had enough of this journey". They feared not reaching land as no sight of land was seen for days and days. It was devastating for these immigrants, and it was havoc aboard. Sanitation was poor, as the Indians had no toilets or shower, and they had to stoop down on deck to relieve themselves. There was no water to bathe properly; only an occasional bucket of sea water. Cholera and dysentery were present as well as other diseases. Among those that survived was my great, great grandfather as the ship traveled on to Trinidad.

Mohammed Moktee stood out among his fellow passengers; he wasn't scared, and the full brunt of the storm did not terrify him. He had made up his mind that he was going forward and was determined to make this journey not as a coward or a trembling bystander. He knew that in the long run he would prosper and his wits and strength would carry him through. At long last the ship arrived in Trinidad, and he and the others who survived were sent to the different estates according to the different identification numbers given out by the overseers. It is clear now that any thought that this voyage was mixed with excitement and romance is not true. Trying to reach a friend or relative, when they reached land, who may have come on a previous voyage, turned into disappointment and frustration. How lucky I am not to be with a crew of wailing people, as I don't know if I could have survived under those terrible conditions. I may even have lost my sanity. The immigrants were surely tired and exhausted aboard this vessel. The conditions were dreadful. The men and women were in cramped, fetid and choking spaces. Quarters below deck were so crowded and had no portholes, little ventilation, and no toilet facilities. Many became desperate. The passengers had to bear the foul smell which was appalling. Many did not wash but remained in the very same garments that they had when they entered the ship. Those that were seasick could not lift up their heads to see anything. Packed in like sardines, they often cried out saying "I want to go home, what a hell this is!" Even eating must have been difficult; even if they felt like eating, they weren't well enough because of the boat rocking and pitching so much. Some starved because they were not able or willing to eat. White bunk beds with white sheets were for the men but the women slept on the floor.

Most of the passengers were infested with lice. They couldn't think straight and prayed for land. The ship rocked with the hurricane in full blast, and many imagined that they would never see land again and gave up hope. The lice seemed to make their lives all the more overbearing and added to their misery. Finally, when the Indians disembarked from the vessels to the docks, there was a cry of relief to see land. Some shouted, "Good riddance to the ocean and the ship, we are glad to get out of here." They scrambled to the train to take them to the sugar plantation depot in Princes Town. At long last they were on their way to a new life. Some of the immigrants exclaimed "Thank God, we are free, we are coming to a new home after that wretched journey." After four months in the open ocean in all kinds of weather, packed together under terrible conditions the journey into a strange land had ended. They were happy to be at their destination.

As soon as the ship was tied to the dock, the Indians gathered their belongings and scrambled down the gang planks to the other end of the dock, across the little town, across the little streets. Here they were assembled at the receiving depot set up to check out the physical wellbeing of the new immigrants. They were tested for diseases and infirmities, which could disqualify them from taking part in the indentured laborer program. If they had any kind of permanent infirmity, they could be held until the next ship came and returned to India without ever working a day. Although this was a possibility, it mostly did not happen, and by far most of the laborers were assembled and stood up among the various plantation owners who had applied for labor. They were taken to the various sugar plantations. After four months of being on the open ocean, they were certainly glad to be on solid ground once again, although they did not know what life would turn out to be like in this strange new land.

They tried to be optimistic and look forward to working and completing their contract. I am sure most felt they would be going back to India at the end of their five years with money in their pockets.

The Arrival

Mohammed Moktee and future wife Modea likely came on the same ship *Equestrian* which landed on the docks at Port of Spain, Trinidad in March, 1852. They traveled first to the depot at Princes Town. There they changed to mule carts for the last ten to twelve miles out to the sugar plantations known as the Garth Estate. Moktee, like all other indentured laborers, had to cut and load canes onto mule carts. A food ration in the form of rice and flour was delivered to the plantation once a week. The indentured laborers were paid the equivalent of about 25 cents a day for their work but many still managed to save a portion for themselves or send some back home to India. The conditions in the barracks were poor. The workers were given a "Chula" (brick oven) for cooking, but mostly they slept on the floor. The rooms were dirty and smelled terribly. They were infested with chiggers and head lice. Bed bugs and other insects made life miserable for the workers. They bit them and feasted on their blood during the night. At night some of the workers would curse and quarrel; some would wake up in the middle of the night crying loudly. The infested barracks made the Indians cry out saying, "We want to go back to India." Life was certainly no bed of roses, but perhaps more disgusting, a bed of bugs. Moktee heard all of this and tried to console them, saying, "Better days are coming. We are going to build a new life; do not worry. Just have some patience." Though Moktee felt the same pain as they did, he had to show them he was strong and courageous and that they should not give up hope.

Occasionally, Indians might be beaten if they refused to work well in the fields, but Moktee had the strength and dignity to forget the reprimands and worked diligently. He felt that he must go on regardless of all the trials and tribulations that he faced. There was no turning back now so he vowed to make the best of it. Once Moktee started working in the cane fields, he began to visualize that the day would come when he would be a free man. This made him continue to work even harder at his job.

Ancestors

My Great, Great Grandfather (Mohammed Moktee)
The history of this family begins in 1851 when a twenty year-old man, Mohammed Moktee, signed the indenture papers and left on a four-month journey on the ocean to Trinidad. My great, great grandfather Moktee was

excited. He was relieved and courageous to withstand the fear and hardship on the vessel. But there was no turning back for him. Moktee went directly to the Garth Estate in Mission Village on March 27, 1852.

He was unlike most other plantation workers. He worked his way up in the plantation workforce, and in a few years married Modea. After he had finished his period of indentureship, Mohammed Moktee decided to start his own business. (Most just did their work without ambition to move on or to change their lives by planning for a better life.) They had seven children, all of whom were girls. After Moktee's indentureship, through hard work and perseverance, he became a wealthy man and he insisted that his children be educated by a teacher. The sisters all had entrepreneurial skills as well.

Sapoojahn, one of his daughters was far cleverer than her sisters and was such an astute and accomplished pupil that Moktee was especially fond of her. She was, as they say, the "apple of his eye," and his favorite child. She was the one who excelled. His fourth daughter, Sapoojahn, called Sapoo, was born on April 23, 1869, in the village of Princes Town. Her birth was registered on page 374 of the 1869 Register in the district of Sande Grande. Altogether, they had seven daughters: Lutchmeejahn followed by Nobiejahn, then Bebeejahn, Sapoojahn-my great grandmother-, Sookejahn, Neykeejahn and Mereejahn. Seven daughters and no sons.

By the time his first daughter Lutchmeejahn was ready to get married, probably about fifteen years later, (in 1875) he had enough money that he was able to pay off the young groom's contract. According to Shamshu Deen who wrote the book, <u>Solving East Indian Roots in Trinidad,</u> Mohammed Moktee became a wealthy man in Mission Village and was looking around for a suitable groom for his first daughter Lutchmeejahn. He went around to various estates seeking out an educated Muslim man. He was pleased to meet one Moulvi Mohammed John at the Brothers Estate. Moktee was attracted by the brilliance of this young man and approached him with the proposition: "If you marry my daughter, I will pay off your indenture contract." This was agreed, and Mohammed John married Lutchmeejahn.

In January of 1878, Mohammed John and Lutchmeejahn had a son. The birth was recorded by Mohammed Moktee himself, who was listed as a shopkeeper. Obviously, being a shopkeeper was the source of Mohammed Moktee's wealth. Moktee was not only wealthy, he was also innovative. He had developed what was at that time, an advanced system of transportation from Sande Grande to San Fernando. He had imported dozens of mules and ran a caravan using mule carts. There is an interesting story about this mule cart business. When the government realized how profitable the enterprise was, they sent government veterinarians who tested the mules and diagnosed all of Moktee's mules with a deadly virus. They ordered all the animals to be destroyed. Soon after, the government had other people start their own mule transportation business, which was so successful that it later evolved into a railroad. For some strange but obvious reason all of Moktee's mules had this deadly illness, but the government people's mules were fine. Isn't that amazing? A bit too amazing perhaps.

According to Jean Fitz Charles, granddaughter of Lutchemeejahn, Moktee was also a successful landowner in the heart of Mission Village. In the 1860s and 1870s Mohammed Moktee bought many pieces of land in Sande Grande where he lived. From the 1860s to the 1880s Mohammed Moktee and his lands prospered with the rise of business and wealth in San Fernando and in Mission Village. The tram road was extended, new businesses, lumber sales, new estates, and farms were opening up, and new towns and villages were linked to the East coast of Trinidad. The Trinidad Royal Gazette made several references in the 1870s to Moktee as a successful shopkeeper. Between 1877 and 1879 Moktee owned and operated as many as three shops simultaneously, and, in 1879, the Royal Gazette showed Moktee as operating three liquor shops.

Moktee served his five years diligently to get out of the cane field work, which he despised tremendously. Success was his goal, and his business talent made him a wealthy man. He was a profitable shopkeeper and ran a transportation system using mule carts, even though the government closed this enterprise because of his prosperity. Over time, others ran the same business, but failed. The government was foolish to justify their action against Moktee. My great, great grandfather saw the advantage of owning several properties in Mission Village. He invested in these properties because the village was growing more rapidly than other surrounding places. Vendors would set up stands selling refreshments to passengers at the terminal in Mission Village. He was clever and made even more money because of his insight in business. Concerts, brass-bands, minstrels, and solo artists provided entertainment at the terminal, and he took his family to many of these engagements.

It was quoted in *The Royal Gazette* in 1870 that my great, great grandfather, a successful landowner and businessman with class and distinction, had a leading role to play in the prosperity of Mission Village. He created a bit of history by fulfilling his contract and also by showing that he could trade the past for a rewarding future. Mohammed Moktee was definitely an important man to my roots. Moktee vowed that he would never go back to the cane fields after his indentureship. He worked harder than any of the others and took pride and diligence with his work from morning to evening. He was a survivor, a hard and honest worker with no time even to take his meals decently.

My Great, Grand-mother (Sapoojahn)

Sapoojahn, one of his daughters was far cleverer than her sisters and was such an astute and accomplished pupil that Moktee was especially fond of her. She was, as they say, the "apple of his eye," his favorite child. She was the one who excelled. His fourth daughter, Sapoojahn, called Sapoo, was born on April 23, 1869, in the village of Princes Town. Her birth was registered on page 374 of the 1869 Register in the district of Sande Grande.

Mohammed Moktee was 38 years old when Sapoojahn was born on April 23, 1869. At the age of five, Sapoo was taught by a teacher hired by the family. An Indian by birth , he had changed his name from Munradin to John Morton to be more "English." John Morton spoke Urdu and Hindi as well as English and was also a teacher for the Canadian Presbyterian church. John Morton was employed as a teacher for Sapoo and her sisters, as he was qualified in his profession. All the children took a liking to John Morton, and he taught them to read and write and do mathematical calculations. This was instrumental in Sapoojahn becoming a shrewd businesswoman later on, even before her marriage. Sapoojahn was an especially good student. Sapoojahn's early years were like those of any middle class young woman-there were family gatherings, birthdays, picnics, etc.

Sapoo's Marriage to Ghool Khan

When she was fifteen or sixteen years old, Sapoojahn's father, Mohammed Moktee, found an excellent young man with a good family for her to marry. He found Ghool Khan. Later Sapoo and Ghool Khan decided to go into business for themselves. They opened a shop that sold small pastries and sweet drinks with delicious tropical fruit flavors.

The shop became very successful, but the hours were long and hard. The shop was a great success for many years, but when Sapoo was only twenty nine-years old, her beloved husband died. He left Sapoojahn and four children. After the death of Ghool Khan, Sapoo's life became a living hell. There is no pain like the loss of a partner and husband. She felt numb and went into a depression. She took care of the children, the sweet drink factory, and got involved in properties. She had to keep busy and was determined to be a successful business woman. But she started to drink without anyone knowing, to kill her pain. This helped for a time, but would prove to be a very difficult medicine to stop. It is often true that people who have been scarred by a violent or unhappy marriage are usually reluctant to risk another. But those who have been happy together, and who have tasted spiritual and physical togetherness instinctively long for it again. Sapoojahn missed the presence of her husband. Some relatives hit upon the idea that she should remarry. After all, she was self sufficient and would be no burden for a new husband. When this was first suggested she resisted the idea of marrying again. No one else could take the place of Ghool. She was on her own. She was a wealthy and independent widow. But a meeting was arranged by her friends and relatives between Sapoo and Abdul Ghany, a very fair and handsome man, educated, but not as well off as Sapoo financially.

Sapoo's Second Marriage to Abdul Ghany

When Sapoo first set eyes on Abdul, she became mesmerized by his good looks. He would soon become her knight in shining armor. Abdul knew that Sapoo was wealthy and he saw an opportunity through her to become wealthy, too, if they formed a union. The only sort of union that would join them was marriage, and so Abdul married Sapoo. Sapoo was never very beautiful. Clever, yes, but she stood out because of her kind nature and good manners. She spoke like a lady, and she kept herself groomed at all times. She copied the clothing of the missionaries. She started to wear European clothes at an early age. She wore stockings and leather shoes and white blouses with long black skirts. The only similar piece of clothing worn by the laborers was an "orhrini" or white scarf to cover her head. This woman could read and write fluent English and was a clever businesswoman which made her powerful to her friends and husband. A photograph of her shows her in a resplendent outfit. It was taken in a studio. As a child,

I used to look at this photograph and marvel that this was Trinidad in the early part of the twentieth century. Sapoojahn was already middle-aged but she had an air of dignity and class about her.

Sapoojahn's Secret

After the death of Ghool Khan, Sapoo found a bit of romance with her new husband Abdul and she was thrilled with the idea that he adored her and praised her for being a successful woman. He told her that the women he had known could not stand up to her. Sapoo had began drinking while still married to Ghool, and still drank surreptiously. Abdul had no idea that she was drinking because it was done behind his back. Alcohol made her feel good and less depressed, and her problems seem to go away. According to family history, Sapoo had a profitable sweet drink shop in Princes Town which she later moved with her new husband to Curepe. With the income she had, she could afford a teacher for her children and was a moderately wealthy lady. She was fashion-conscious and drove a buggy to town to buy whatever was needed. She looked like some of the other rich women. She was indeed vain and never wanted to remember the cane field stories that her father had told her about. Sapoo had six children with Ghool Khan and seven with Abdul Ghany. She ultimately died during childbirth while she was still not very old. Abdul Ghany, in turn, took a new wife and eventually had seven more children. Fortunately, Abdul was able financially to provide well for all the children.

My Grandfather Shah

When I was a child, I was completely mesmerized by the tales my aunts told, especially those told by my adopted aunt Doris. She was the daughter of a Negro servant who died while in employment, and my grandfather agreed to let my grandmother bring her up because he was led to believe she was the daughter of one of his own daughters who had made the mistake of having an affair with a servant.

I recall Aunt Doris (for that is what we were told to call her) well. She would spin long stories of my Dada, that is, my grandfather Mohammed Shah Khan. She would often refer to him as "Cusrew"- a self-styled man, well mannered, and always well groomed with his beard trimmed. He dressed like royalty. I am told everyone called him Cusrew, and he took delight in explaining that "Cusrew" behaved like a real King. My grandfather was very fair and having been taught by the Canadian Missionaries to read and write English, considered himself a scholar. It was he who led his whole generation and us his grandchildren to believe that our ancestors came from the Indian frontier near Afghanistan. He told his children that that they were the descendents of the Pathans, that the name Khan is Pathan and that they came from a long line of warriors. There was even speculation that the family was descended from Ghengis Khan. Perhaps it was true; he was also fair in color and being very proud and vain, he did not or could not associate himself with the "coolies" who had come to Trinidad to work under the indentured labor system. It was only when I grew up and researched my family' history that I learned that my ancestors came from a small place called Pathna in Bihar in Central India, one of the poorest parts of India, and nowhere near Afghanistan.

Shah lived in a dream world. He would attire himself in the clothes of an English Gentleman and played the game of "drafts" for hours on end with friends. He entertained his friends by singing and playing the harmonica and took a delight in making them laugh with his remarkable wit. All these frivolities went on while his buggies were hired out. It was mostly during those occasions he would tell all the men in the community who came to sit and play draft with him of the great and historical lives of his ancestors- the Pathans. And so word got around that his family came from a long line of Afghan warriors. All the men in the village looked up to him because he could read and write, and he would assist some of them to fill out their forms for various small claims.

As a teenager, my grandfather Shah Khan drove a bus which his parents bought, and he earned a fair wage doing so. It was hard work taking passengers from the village to rural areas and making many trips, but he wanted to show his parents that nothing was too hard for him. He realized that his parents still had not forgotten the system of indentureship embodied in their souls, and so he vowed that he must look forward to a better life. My grandfather was also a very good hunter. He had well-trained hunting dogs and frequently returned with deer and other animals. Not only did he hunt, but he was also an outdoor man with an interest in breeding cows, which were milked and sold to the villagers in the market. Lying around him amidst the green grass of his backyard were cows, goats and an old mule. They were his companions after a hard day's work. He transported the living, and sometimes, even the dead, to the country. He never mentioned the latter to anyone. My older sister, Nisa, recalls how he used to read everything to all the older children including stories from the Bible. He would stop at some interesting point so they could not wait until the next day to hear him continue, but of course they did.

When the first Prime Minister of Indian descent in Trinidad went to Bihar to find his long-lost relatives, he was taken there by helicopter and donated thousands of rupees to the villagers. As my childhood was spent thinking of Afghanistan as my mother-country, I would ask various members and elders of the family to tell me more about this country which I felt was part of my life. My generation believed we were somehow superior to the ordinary Indian because we believed we had come from Afghanistan and were descended from warriors.

Later on I realized that my grandfather's tales were not true. He got carried away and he did not want to have any part of the fact that his ancestors were wretched indentured laborers brought by the British to work as "coolies" in the sugar plantations. He saw only a picture of remorse and guilt about the near slave-type system that went before him and how his ancestors suffered, working their lives away under an oppressive contract. He wanted very desperately to forget those stories told to him. He made up this kind of fantasy tale that he was from Afghanistan and not from Bihar. He was as proud as a peacock to tell us these things and never changed his opinions.

Chapter 8

MY FAMILY

Early life of My Father Mohammed Hakim Khan

My father was born in the old city, Port of Spain. He had his high school education in nearby St. Joseph. His conduct and attendance was excellent. He started his career as a dry goods salesman, and later was the general floor manager of J.T. Johnson, a well-known department store in Port of Spain. Son of Mohammed Shah Khan, both he and his father were active members of the local Islamic Association, which was founded in the 1890's. He held the post of Assistant Secretary around 1928.

The Muslims of St. Joseph decided one day to finally erect a Mosque in St. Joseph. My father was given this assignment because of all the work and time he had devoted to the people's dream of having a place of worship in the community instead of going far away to another Mosque. He was a founding member and the first President of the Trinidad Muslim League Mosque. During the Second World War my father was appointed Sub-Warden and later was granted an honorable discharge from the civil defense forces dated 10/24/1944. In addition, that same year, he was elected Secretary of the Indian Welfare Association. In June 1945, my dad organized a conference at the India Club. The purpose of this meeting was to support the removal of the language qualification for voting. Many Indians, of course, spoke in their native languages and could not pass a test given in English. The Government's Legislative Council had recommended that the language test be continued.

At the conference he stated that, "a denial of franchise to persons unable to understand the English Language would be contrary to the spirit of Indentured Immigration to Trinidad". He said that continuation of such legislation would also be detrimental to the political and economic interests of many of the inhabitants of the country. My father remained an active member of the India Club until India's Independence in 1947. In 1947, at the time when India was about to achieve its independence from England, there was much division in India between the various religious groups, chiefly the Hindus and the Muslims, about the terms of Independence and the amount of political power of each group. In Trinidad, because of the many Indians living there, a split also developed within the Indian community, based chiefly on the same religious grounds. In his articles in 1946 and 1947, my father actually got into a bit of trouble with the Indian Muslim League in Trinidad because of his outspoken devotion to the idea that both Hindus and Muslims should act together as one group to celebrate Indian Independence Day in Trinidad and not divide into religious factions as they had done in India.

Mohammed Hakim Khan was the founder, writer, and editor of a quarterly magazine: Al Azan (the Call.) In this publication, he gave his personal opinions and thoughts to readers, and once got into trouble for this. He wrote an article expressing his view that all members of the Indian Community should join together for the Indian Independence Day Celebrations in 1947 in Trinidad rather than have separate Hindu and Muslim celebrations. Hindu leaders objected to the idea and sought to raise only the Hindu "flag of India" on Independence Day at the India Club. They wanted to observe Indian Independence as a gesture, but really deep down in their hearts, these leaders wanted recognition only of their own independence, rather than that of all of India. Because of what he stated in his magazine, Al Azan, he was asked by his committee to resign, and this caused a bit of conflict.

My father was opposed to any form of segregation or division of the two cultures, Hindu and Muslim, and called for both to unite and go forward together as one. This led to the birth of the Inter-Religious Associations in Trinidad. My father did not let those who wanted separation to sway his decision. He believed in peace and a common future for all Indian people. He was doing what he thought was right. He was like the rock of Gibraltar in his decision. He devoted his life to this idea, not for fame, but to help organize practical ways for the Islamic Community and all other religions to interact.

In the field of education, my father believed in the Koran's injunction that the pen of the scholar is mightier than the sword of the warrior. He campaigned tirelessly for all schools to be on par with the excellent Christian schools which had been recognized a century before. He also fought for equal rights for women, so that they could be educated, work, or be involved in charitable activities, in accordance with Islamic principles. The central motivation of his life was now Islam, and through this came the building of the mosque. He had turned his life around for this, but the truth is that not every one was happy with his decision. It was very hard on the family. My mother thought that my father should be an ordinary husband and father with an ordinary job; coming home every evening and spending more time with his family. Imagine a household of thirteen children and not giving them the attention they deserved while my mother, a simple uneducated woman, had to care for such a big family. Still she stood by his side.

The Mosque

Situated in the former capital of Trinidad and Tobago amidst the busy traffic of the bus route of the main road there stands a magnificent Mosque which can be compared with those seen around the globe. This beautiful structure is called The Jinnah Memorial Mosque which brings to our mind the glory of Islam and symbolizes our faith and gives praise and thanks to Allah. On the 15th day of August 1947 the Trinidad Muslim League was founded by a group of devoted Muslims who were to carry out the truth of Islam to Islamic and non Islamic people. It was named after a great Muslim statesman one of the founders of Pakistan: Mohammed Ali Jinnah who was indeed a champion leader in his own country.

My father was educated in the Colonial way of life by the British. He learned the Classics: English Literature and British History like Chaucer, Charles Dickens, the Bronte sisters and more. At age 25 he started a wholesale fabric business. At the peak of his success, my father had a calling from Allah. He left his successful business to pursue his dream of building a mosque for the Muslims of his town. (My mother was "upset" but of course she had nothing to say about it.) However, she supported him and stood by his side.

For ten years he raised the money, then set the cornerstone and even got Pakistan's U.S. ambassador to speak at the ceremony.

Hakim Khan believed and obeyed the laws of the Quran, but he befriended a missionary scholar who had slightly different views of the Quran, and was considered a heretic by some strict believers. Dad treated the missionary and his wife like his own family. My father was open minded, intellectual, curious and invited this man to his home because he and his family knew no one. The hospitality shown to this missionary was enough to raise a storm of controversy within Hakim Khan's own Mosque. This stranger had a non-traditional, but still Islamic, view called Ahmadiyya, a splinter movement based in Pakistan.

My dad was shunned by the elders because of the sin of befriending a traveling Islamic scholar who held beliefs which the elders did not like. They considered my dad a traitor for being so open minded. The Mosque elders were so horrified and disrupted by this stranger's teachings that by the time the Mosque was built and ready to have the opening ceremony, my father, a founding member and chief fund raiser, was shunned and advised not to attend the opening ceremonies. My father chose not to attend the ceremony and my family backed him and did not attend either. In the newspaper report documenting the opening of the Mosque and Islamic Cultural Center, the photograph taken in anticipation of the event in the newspaper had Hakim Khan cut out. This man who had devoted almost his whole life; the spiritual, inspirational leader in creating the Mosque was totally insulted. This was a very un-Islamic thing to do to someone who had been so instrumental in the building effort. Even if they didn't like the idea, he was just listening to a different branch or a controversial preacher within the Islamic Religion. The controversy was so great that it created a rift with the people of the Mosque. Hakim Khan felt that the people of the Mosque unjustifiably made it quite clear that he was not one of them; that he was joining a heretical kind of religious splinter group. And so there was a falling out between my father and the leaders of the Mosque.

These so called religious Mosque back-biters made a split with his family and disruptive as it seemed, even some his friends refused to make up with my dad. They had so much animosity, they never gave any of the recognition that my father should have received for building the Mosque.

How things take a turn in life when you think that nothing can. It was my elder sister, Nisa, who forced the newspaper to reprint the correct photograph including Hakim Khan with the admonition and inclusion of his name. The missionary did manage to talk to some of the more intelligent people and it became evident that the Mosque elders were disturbed, maybe scared and challenged by some of the missionary's views, but my father was not disturbed or challenged. He thought that it wasn't a bad thing to discuss topics of religion in an active discussion. In fact, for hundreds of years, the Islamic religion has been known for open and lively discussions on many controversial issues. But it was evident that whatever happened that it was a split with the Khan family on one side and the Mosque elders on the other. It created a rift which still exists, but others on the Islamic Committee acknowledge my father's work and life-long struggle to build his breath-taking Mosque.

My father was a thinker and doer and when it came time to choose between the Mosque leader's close-minded viewpoints or listen to the new missionary, he didn't hesitate and turned his back to these so called fanatic

Mosque people and they in turn their backs against my dad. And now we see the head of the Mosque a man who didn't kick back. He didn't cry about the split, neither did he grieve about it. My father was knowledgeable and felt that he had done the right thing by being open minded and listened to philosophies and thoughts outside of own little town. So he showed an advance level of thinking which is probably in his genes and genes of his family. Hakim must have known that they had betrayed him. He must have known that they had taken out his picture. Was this some kind of revenge for a man who had devoted his time and life to the sole purpose of the Mosque; even to the point of neglecting his family at times? There was no justifiable reason for them to take out his picture. He thought they were his friends, I would have thought so too. It comes to my mind now that if you disagree with somebody, you can talk about it philosophically. Evidently, the elders of the Mosque were totally intolerant. They refused to listen to an outsider's views. They didn't want to have anything to do with a stranger from a far-away land with other opinions. They felt that they knew the way Islam should be. That is in the Quran and surely to listen to an outsider would be a blow to them. They were in a world of their own and they preached the Quran to the Mosque people; and changes from a missionary would alter their little world. In no way am I saying that my dad was the most wonderful man in his decisions but he was alert and liked to be fair.

These were vicious things they did to him which he didn't deserve at all. We wonder whether his friends he had in business and neighbors stuck with him. Did they still continue to be his friends? We don't have any reports that they didn't. Did they pay attention to him, keep his life going? Or was the nature of this religious split just limited to religious activities or Mosque activities. But the point of all of this was my father was not humbled or embarrassed or shamed of any of this. As far we can tell he stuck to his guns. He believed that he was right and went on with his life. As for the missionary, he got a job as an insurance agent, became a rich man and settled down with his family and eventually left Trinidad. In part because of this big split and controversy my father's health was failing and he died a broken hearted man. News of my father's death spread like wildfire far and wide. As the funeral went on its way, people came from all over the island. People came from the Mosque, from the town and from all over the surrounding villages people came. Many, many came to the house, and the yard was thronged with people. Some of these people had heard of my father and never met him, but they came to his funeral.

I remember as a child looking down from our balcony, I could see the funeral on its way to the cemetery with such a long procession following the hearse. I just cried as much for what my mother was going through rather than my father leaving us. I was told by my aunt Doris a few stubborn members of the Mosque had gone to the beach on an excursion, they didn't care, and they were not present to respect the man who had spent so many years with the Mosque. Was this a payback? Or were they thinking that now they could reap the rewards of my father's hard work?

Isn't it strange that a religion which was started by Mohammed was itself a wild and strange idea at one time? Isn't it ironic that it was Mohammed himself who came up with the idea to preach to hundreds of people. And it was he who was so successful in trying to tell people about his new religion. But when a Muslim scholar came to Trinidad, the very same controversy, the very same preaching was not accepted by the same people who accepted Mohammed.

I wonder how it would have been to interview Mohammed after his first day of preaching. I bet he came back tired, hungry and discouraged. He probably told his wife "Oh God, everybody hates me. Nobody likes me. Nobody believes in me. This is going to be a very hard job and some of them even want to lynch me". But obviously that didn't even stop him, he had a mission to do and he did it. Mohammed ended up converting a third of the world.

After the demise of my dad, my mother was in terrible condition. This woman was going through hell and often in her sleep she would call out my father's name begging him to come back. The fear she had of thirteen starving mouths to feed and with no help turned her to drinking. Her talent was to be near her husband in riches and poorness and now what was she supposed to do? She put off doing the household chores, did not pay attention to us as when my father was alive. She was in some sort of trance a lot of the time. Her ability to cope with anything or anyone was gone. Her life was a nightmare to her. Soon after, my eldest brother graduated from school and he became like our father and continued the business much the same way as my dad started out.

My Mother

My mother grew up in the little town of Curepe, an hour and a half drive south of Port of Spain. At a very young age my mother's real parents disappeared for some unknown reason. She was raised by her foster parents. Her foster parents did not abuse her, but they made her a maid, she worked so hard milking cows that working had become her whole life. She was a stranger to them and a stranger in her own house. Soon she left to live with her brother Dan in Curepe. At her brother's house she was much more comfortable, and she kept herself busy-she was a worker bee, and her brother bought her new clothes and treated her well.

My father and his parents happened to live across the street from Dan and his father thought that my mother would make a very good match for him. My dad at that time was working at the J.T. Johnson department store, doing quite well, and mixing with sociable people. My dad's parents noticed the beautiful young woman who had moved in across the street, and noticed that she was a dutiful and a hard worker. They thought that they should ask for her hand in marriage for their son. Of course, there was no need for him to do any actual asking. As was the custom then, and very much to this day, arranged marriages were normal. So they made all the arrangements with the family and my dad soon found himself married to my mother. Although it was an arranged marriage, he never regretted it, for my mother brought him joy and happiness. My father with his new wife lived in Curepe for a while, and came to St. Joseph to live in his parent's house. This was a much larger house with more rooms and a very big backyard. He paid the mortgage, and his parents lived in the lower level. My father took care of his parents and his wife.

My father starting out in Business

My father started his working life as a Sales Assistant in the largest department store in Port of Spain, Trinidad. He was promoted to General Manager of this store called J.T. Johnston Ltd owned by local white/English Trinidadians. He was the first local man who was non-English to be appointed to this post. This was still colonial Trinidad in many ways, and many of the proprietors of stores were from those families who originally came from England. There were also a few industrious Indian men who owned small stores selling merchandise and hardware.

At the age of about forty, my father resigned from J.T. Johnson and opened a small store selling men's clothing in St. Joseph. My aunt Julie used to run the store for him and later on after my eldest sister Shannon graduated from a finishing school run by French Canadian nuns, she also helped to run the store. My father had taken to the road as a salesman in a van. Day after day he would pack the van and drive to far places in the south of Trinidad where he would sell his goods as a wholesaler to small shops in the rural areas. His customers all respected him and he would allow them credit which they paid off in installments. He soon became well off and he bought the large old colonial type house from his parents. In addition to paying them, he looked after them until their demise. My father then re-built the house and while it was being built we all moved into a small house in the village of Curepe. Because there were so many children, my father built a very large, beautiful home with three verandas all around, a large drawing room, a dining room and a library. In that library is a hand-built mahogany book case filled with books he had purchased and collected. They are still there to this day- all of Charles Dickens novels and books like Gibbons-The Fall of The Roman Empire, the works of Plato and many history books.

He had erected a large gymnasium at the rear end of the large back yard for us to play in and this was used sometimes to entertain friends and visitors whenever there was a banquet. Tables were temporarily put up and decorated with flowers between serving plates. My father was a very outgoing man and he entertained his guests on a grand scale. Cooks were hired to prepare the meal and my elder sisters would help to decorate the tables with flowers and fine Irish linen napkins. There were always at least three courses. Once or twice a year my father would invite all the poor people in the town of St. Joseph and nearby areas for lunch. My mother would do the cooking and my father would assist her. All the children who were old enough had to serve the poor people personally. We were told we would receive the blessings of Allah if we were kind to the poor. Then my father would give each guest a little money or "satka" and they would say a short prayer to bless our home. I was a child then but I remembered this celebration and how much it meant to my father to feed the poor.

Our home was always beautifully and tastefully decorated. My father himself would choose the curtains and upholstery for the mahogany three piece suite in the living room. There were two large mahogany tables-one in the main dining room and one in the back veranda for the younger children who were too small to sit on chairs. Some of us sat on a long bench. It was a little uncomfortable but we had no choice. There was always a servant to take care of us, as far back as I can recall. There was one Negro lady called Sidrin who is still alive and whenever I go back to Trinidad I would always go and look for her. "My-my, how you have grown up Zobi" she would say and hug me. It is strange but all my parents children share a common trait-they are all house-proud-even the males in the family. My younger brother Afzal who acts as a custodian now that most of us are away has added chandeliers, mirrors and Chinese rugs sent by Nisa from Harrod's in London, for the house. Nisa had purchased two full china dinner service sets, china tea sets and other ornaments.

My mother used to refer to them as "wares" and could not believe that a single plate could cost $16US or about $100 Trinidad dollars. But she too soon grew accustomed to using fine china and in a mahogany front glassed cupboard, some of them are locked away-only to be used when visitors or any one of us from abroad return home. One of my sister's, Zeeni, also built an elegant bungalow for her family in Westmoorings- one of the upscale areas in Trinidad. She still advises Afzal on the decorations of our home and assists him to keep it looking beautiful-for that is how everyone describes our home.

My father had always said that it is essential to have a home and a roof over one's head and because there were so many children, he asked that the house should never be sold in the event one of us had to return home. My father had seen "Gone with the Wind" and he called our home "Tara". As mentioned above, my great, great-grandfather Moktee was an indentured laborer, and my dad heard the stories of indentureship from his grandfather and father. The memories of indentureship were in the distant past, but not forgotten. However, a new life and a new period was about to begin in the time and life of Mohammed Hakim Khan.

Building a Mosque

In 1947, India got it's independence from Britain and the new state of Pakistan came into being. Many thousands of lives were lost during the emigration of nearly all who decided to make a new life in Pakistan. The Trinidad Muslim League was formed under the guidance of my father and two friends. It's main aim and object was to build a Mosque for the Muslim community of St. Joseph and champion the cause of the Muslim women in order that they should have more freedom in public life. My father's teachings included "Muslim women taking part in public life, entering professions and appearing in radio and television." Education was to be the main theme for Muslim women. My father's first venture in this respect was to send two of my sisters to a colonial high school.

They were probably the first two Muslim young children to attend the well known Bishop Anstey High School in Port of Spain; an Anglican based institution run by teachers from England, Ireland and New Zealand.

Around this time a parcel of land was acquired in St. Joseph for the purpose of erecting a "dream mosque" which came to fruition years later. It came to the attention of The Trinidad Muslim League that the very first Ambassador of the newly formed State of Pakistan was appointed to represent Pakistan in Washington, USA. An invitation was hastily sent out by The Trinidad Muslim League to the Pakistan authorities in Pakistan asking for the Ambassador to stop over on his way to Washington for a day or so, for the sole purpose of laying the foundation stone on the proposed site for the Mosque. It was agreed the Mosque would be named after the first president of Pakistan, Mohammed Ali Jinnah. The invitation was accepted by the Pakistan Government and so the designated ambassador, Mr.Espahani broke his journey and stopped over in Trinidad for this momentous event.

The Muslim community felt honored to have the newly appointed Ambassador lay the foundation stone for the proposed mosque. The local community came out in large numbers to welcome this dignitary. As the land was bare a small tent was erected and chairs were placed on a platform for the committee members and the dignitary to sit. The women folk catered for this occasion by providing delicacies and soft drinks for everyone.

My father had arranged for my sister Nisa to place a garland around Ambassador Espahani's neck upon his arrival. Welcome speeches were made and the Ambassador returned this compliment in appreciation after he laid the foundation stone. A plaque marks the spot to this day. Apparently, the Ambassador was very impressed with the Muslim community of Trinidad. It was proposed to name the future mosque after the first President of Pakistan, Mohammed Ali Jinnah. Obviously, he reported all these events in Trinidad to the higher authorities in Pakistan who were also very impressed and to this day there is a special relationship between Pakistan and Muslim Trinidadians.

As the years went by, various missionaries from Pakistan came to Trinidad to spread the teachings of Islam and they were all welcomed. For several years my father and some of his colleagues worked very hard to raise building funds for the mosque by organizing bazaars, fetes, singing contests towards this aim. Finally, after being shown photographs of some of the most beautiful mosques in the Middle East, together with the architect my father and the committee members decided upon the design of the mosque to be built.

My father was instrumental in purchasing most of the building materials from a local supplier called William H. Scott Ltd. My father was a good customer of William H. Scott. The proprietor Mr. Scott himself agreed to hire my brother Baita who was taken to meet Mr. Scott. My brother at the age of seventeen had acquired excellent credits in the Cambridge Overseas School Certificate Examination and Mr. Scott immediately hired him. To this day after many years, my brother is still employed by that company and has been elevated to the post of Manager. William H. Scott now has grown from a small company into a million dollar hardware company. Mr. Scott senior, has since passed away and his sons have asked my brother to stay on with the company even after retiring age and he is still with that company today.

I want to mention that when the Mosque was being built, my father would spend long hours on the site discussing the project with contractors, builders and workmen and he would often come home late at night. In addition to having built a very large home for my mother and the children and trading as a wholesale merchant, I often wonder how he found the time to spend on so many unrelated projects. In fact, I have been told that a senior lecturer at the University College of the West Indies - Dr. Brinsley Samaroo, is researching material to write a book on a Muslim pioneer of that era with my father as the main subject. Dr. Samaroo interviewed my sister Nisa in London and told her he often wondered how a man like my father found the time to complete all these projects, edit a magazine and write books and short stories.

Family Portrait

I want to add to this discussion a rather interesting tale about my family life. My father was a devout Muslim who built, almost single-handedly, a mosque in his hometown of St. Joseph. My father, who was a mostly self-taught man, recognized the advantages of providing his children with a proper Western education and encouraged them to succeed in whatever they did. My father had read the classics and was fond of Kipling, Dickens, the Bronte Sisters, and Jane Austen. He edited a local monthly magazine. I remember, as a schoolgirl, how he read to me an account of the hardships suffered by his own grandparents under the Indian Indentured System of Trinidad.

My father began business as a small wholesaler selling clothing and fabric to the rich and poor. He became a successful merchant who created a small business out of nothing but hard work and a persuasive personality. He was generous to the poor, humble, and trustworthy. He was never arrogant, and the more he saw of poverty, the more charitable he became. My father built a house for my mother and a family of thirteen children. He had fun with his children, and took them out to picnics and bazaars and to the seaside on weekends. I remember the glorious days of cricket matches he took us all to see, when Trinidad played against England or Pakistan or India. Then suddenly, just when everything was going well, he announced to my mother his intention to build a mosque for the local community, that they needed a place of worship and that he would do Allah's work. Perhaps he didn't realize that he would need to devote the rest of his life to this cause.

What sparked my dad to do this? I can only assume that being successful as a provider he saw the opportunity to help other people. Aside from being kind and charitable, it must take courage to even suggest such an idea. His great desire to push ahead was truly outstanding, to give up a comfortable life and struggle to get financial help. It wasn't exactly easy. Some of his friends, whom he had known and trusted for many years, turned their backs on him. Some thought he was going crazy and refused to help. It must have been difficult for him to beg, time and time again, to get money from all around, and to travel from village to village in order to start this project. But with his wits, integrity, and his charm, he started on this difficult journey.

With the natural resistance of people to help, setting about to build the mosque was not easy. My mother wasn't happy either, with thirteen children to care for, and so many responsibilities ahead for her. She wondered how she could help to support the family with such little education while her husband gave up his business and devoted his life to his important project. It was hard on my mother to raise the children on her own. It was indeed hard on the whole family. But Dad felt that it was Allah's work. He provided for the family but continued to do what he felt had to be done for the poor people who wanted a place of worship.

Even my mother's good sense of humor couldn't bring him to change his mind! Her devotion as a good wife and mother to so many children seemed not only an extraordinary burden, but now an impossible one. She relied on him for supporting the family, and she feared if he did take on such a task it would mean that there would be a cut in household expenditures and less money to put food on the table and other expenses. My mother was worried, but she could not stand in his way. She didn't fight him tooth and nail, but said that it was Allah's work and that she accepted her husband's decision and would make the best of it. This mission became the central thing in his life. He was totally committed to answering the call from Allah to devote his life to such a worthy cause. Thinking back, I remember that even at an early age this event created some interesting stories in our house. There were arguments between my mother and father, about how this idea came about. Mama knew that she would have to give the children much more attention, and she worried about the additional responsibilities that she would now have to handle. She was a mother of thirteen children, with little education, and she did not understand why her husband had to do something like this. It was not a revelation; he was not struck by lightning. He was a sensible, understanding man who made a good living. He wanted to do something worthy for his people. He was not pretentious and he mixed with both the rich and poor. He poured out his heart and asked all to help toward support of this project, so that the Muslim community could have its own place of worship. Also, my dad contributed financially by giving his own money toward the setting of the foundation. Because of this financial burden my mother began cutting back on family spending.

Pioneer

The Muslims of St. Joseph decided to hold a meeting at Ramgoolie Hall, in Curepe, and voted to erect a mosque in St. Joseph. My father was put in charge of this assignment because of all the work and time he had devoted to the dream of having a place of worship in the local community instead of having to go so far away to another mosque. It usually takes one kind of person to build a building, and quite a different kind of person to be a preacher. Builders are not generally preachers. A builder organizes and makes things happen and hires workers to do the job and everything else in construction. My father had this ability not only to be a builder, but when the mosque was finished, he became a preacher as well. The mosque became his second home. He spent long hours there and at various places about the island, teaching the people about Islam.

In my father's magazine Al Azan, he made the point that acting together meant Muslims accepting the fact that there were a lot of Hindus celebrating with them. Altogether, he said, it was a much more useful thing for all the Indians of Trinidad to stick together and become one Indian culture, rather than appear to be a divided nation to the others in Trinidad. My father's magazine, Al Azan was written chiefly by him and run from his home.

Going through the various issues of that paper, one could see that he addressed a wide range of national and international issues written in the magazine for the education and knowledge of the Muslim community to which he was so devoted. Many of my dad's papers contain hand-written short stories, which will be published at some future time. Although my father was a devout Muslim and a leader of the community, he was extremely interested and persuasive in the area of women's education and women's rights, and in the improvement of children's work conditions. Many of the women in the community have benefited directly from the things that my father started back in 1947, because of his emphasis on equal education and on creating opportunities for women to get ahead and become doctors, lawyers, or any other profession or occupation. The Trinidad Muslim League was very successful in promoting Muslim society in Trinidad. At the 40th anniversary celebration in 1987, the President of Trinidad and Tobago offered congratulations to the league and its founders. He said that my father was not only one of the Pioneers of the League, but was indeed the very driving force behind it, leading to the building of the first mosque in St. Joseph, called the Jinnah Memorial Mosque.

The Controversy

Mohammed Hakim worked for many years to raise the money for the new mosque. He was a pioneer and the first leader of The Jinnah Memorial Mosque. He was a born leader. According to Nisa Khan, his daughter the lawyer, there came a time when a religious leader with somewhat different Islamic beliefs came from Pakistan to Trinidad to preach his concept of the Qu'ran. In the Muslim religion, as in other religions, there are splinter groups with new and unaccepted ideas and controversies that always crop up, and they are all considered. In Christianity they would call them heresies or religious groups with different beliefs. According to my sister Nisa, the mention of the word "Ahmadi" in Pakistan was enough to get one arrested, maybe put in jail, or possibly worse. It was said that Mirza Gulam Ahmad, who was the founder of the Ahamadi movement in Pakistan, was called an impostor by many people.

Around this time and during the building of the mosque, a missionary from Lahore, Pakistan, arrived in Trinidad with his wife and children to stay. My father befriended him like most visitors from Pakistan and offered him hospitality. The missionary, Moulvi Saqui, had no home. My father found accommodation for this Moulvi, his wife and young children. His wife Bahin did not speak any English and wore a burkha, a piece of wood to which a veil was attached. Often they would be invited to our home to share main meals with us and this continued until they managed to set up a little home of their own with some home appliances. My father who always showed an interest in the teachings of Islam would give Moulvi

Saqui a hearing at all times. My father soon learned that Moulvi Saqui belonged to the Ahmadiya movement in Pakistan. At first my father was a bit troubled because the Ahmadiya movement in Pakistan was criticized and members were ostracized by other Muslims. The Ahmadis were persecuted, reviled, spat upon and sometimes killed because they were considered heretics. Although he wasn't leaving the Islamic religion or joining any other religion, my father's hospitality to this man was enough to raise a storm of controversy within his own mosque.

Although the new preacher believed as they all did, that Mohammed was the last prophet of God, he also preached the Ahmadi view that from time to time a "reformer" would arise to remind the people of Islam and its teachings. But this was very controversial, because any "reformer" might be considered the same as a modern day "prophet". But Mohammed was fundamentally held to be the "last prophet." Any belief that someone might come after Mohammed would be extremely difficult, even dangerous. Now, the leaders of the Mosque were so horrified and disrupted by this missionary's teachings that by the time the mosque was built and ready to have the opening ceremonies, Hakim Khan, the pillar of the community, was not able to attend these ceremonies. This man, who made it all happen, was either not allowed to attend the opening ceremonies or he chose not to attend. His whole family backed him and did not attend either. According to Nisa Khan, in the newspaper reports documenting the opening of the new Mosque and Islamic Cultural Center, the photograph used in anticipation of the event and to be used in the newspaper coverage, had Hakim Khan's picture cut out. This was a photograph of Hakim Khan, the spiritual leader, and the secretary standing on the empty site of where the mosque was going to be built. This was totally insulting to his contribution and seemingly a very un-Islamic thing to do. It was extremely hurtful to someone who had been so instrumental in creating the Mosque, even if they didn't like the idea that he was listening to a different branch of Islam or a controversial preacher within the Islamic religion. When the senior members of the Trinidad Muslim League heard that my father was hospitable to Moulvi Saqui who was an Ahmadi, they objected strongly to my father's association with this man. Some accused my father of being an Ahamadi himself. My father was hospitable to almost anyone he met and being sympathetic to Moulvi Saqui did not in any way imply to anyone that he was an Ahmadi.

The controversy was so intense that it created a rift between the people of the Mosque and my family. My dad felt that the people of the Mosque did not want him to attend, that they felt that he was no longer one of them, and was joining a heretical kind of religion or religious splinter group. So there was a falling out between Hakim Khan and his own Mosque. How things take a turn in life when you think that nothing can! Surely this was a disruptive time. Hakim really never made amends with the others and they never gave the recognition that Hakim Khan should have received for building the Mosque.

My sister Nisa did say that during one of her visits to Trinidad she literally forced the Gazette newspaper to reprint the correct photograph to include Hakim Khan with the inclusion of his name. Finally he received some justice done on his side to prove that he was instrumental in the building of the Mosque, however, previously the mosque leaders had rewritten history like dictators do and "included him out." Through this great effort, Nisa had corrected the error.

Nisa said that this was a matter of a simple guru or preacher of high renown who came to Trinidad and gave his views on religious subjects which were all within the Islamic religion and not outside. But it was a controversy far from Hakim's native land. With his superior knowledge he was able to talk to some of the more intelligent people clearly but totally within the bounds of the Islamic religion. It is clear now that the people of the Mosque were disturbed and maybe scared and challenged by some of the preaching.

But Mr. Khan was not disturbed or challenged. He was interested, and thought that it was not a bad thing to openly discuss the topic of religion in an active discussion. In fact, for hundreds of years, the Islamic religion has been known for open discussion. But it is clear that whatever happened, there was a split with the Khan family on one side and the Mosque administration on the other. It created a split and a controversy which still exists, even though Nisa has forced the other people to acknowledge my father's work and life-long struggle to build that mosque. Hakim Khan was instrumental within his own mosque in promoting the education of women and young girls, calling it acceptable. A few disliked the idea, but they could not argue with him because it was mentioned in the Qur'an itself. He was also interested in voting rights and making sure that all people could vote including women. Hakim Khan was a thinker and a doer.

When it came time to choose between the mosque and freedom of speech, he did not hesitate one bit: he turned his back as on the intolerant as they had turned their backs on him. He didn't kick back, he didn't cry about it, neither did he grieve about it. He went about his life assured in the knowledge that he had done the right thing by being open-minded. He listened to philosophies and thoughts outside of his own little town. He showed an advanced level of thinking which reflected the thoughtfulness of his ancestral legacy. Hakim must have known that some people in the town had betrayed him. He must have known that they removed his picture. Was this some kind of revenge they had for a man who neglected his family in order to devote his time and life to the sole purpose of the mosque?

There was no justifiable reason for the newspaper to remove his picture. Hakim surely would have preferred an open forum to discuss the tension that was brewing. These were vicious things that the town did to him, which he did not deserve at all. We wonder whether his business friends and neighbors stuck with him. Did they still continue to be his friends? We have no reports that they did not. Did they pay attention to him, keep his life going? Or was the nature of this religious split just limited to religious activities or mosque activities? The point of all of this is that my father was not humbled or embarrassed or shamed by any of this; as far as we can tell, he stuck to his guns; he believed he was right, and he went on with his life.

As for the missionary himself, he got a job as an insurance agent, became a successful man, and settled down with his family. But later, he left the island of Trinidad. We don't know if he ever made peace with the mosque or if he was accepted by the mosque. I was told by my aunt Doris that because of this big split and controversy, when my father died, a certain few members of the Mosque went on a trip to the beach. They were not present to pay their respects to the man with whom they had spent so many years building the mosque. Was this some kind of a payback, or were they thinking that now they could reap the rewards of my father's hard work? News of my father's death spread like wildfire. As the funeral went on its way, people came from far and wide all over the island of Trinidad.

People came from all over; from the mosque, the town, and the surrounding villages. Many came to the house, and the yard was thronged with people. Some of these people had heard of my father but had never met him, yet they came to his funeral. I looked down from our balcony, and I could see the on its way to the cemetery with such a long procession following the hearse. I cried just as much for what my mother was going through as for my father leaving us. She was in a terrible condition.

I would often wake up to hear my mother saying in her sleep, "Hako, Hako, come back. Don't leave me with all these children to take care of. I need you, Hako." My mother could not accept that my father was dead. She never really got over it. She would go about doing the household chores as though in a trance. At times, particularly late in the evening, she would cry, the tears coming down her face like a drop from a leaking tap. Back then there was no psychologist to help heal her wounds, and so she lived on with his memories and with us.

I thought it strange that all this could occur within a religion started by Mohammed, who himself came up with the wild and strange idea to preach to hundreds of people and was so successful in telling people about his new idea of religion. But when one of his scholars came to Trinidad, the very same controversy, the very same preaching, is now not accepted by the same people who accepted Mohammed.

I wonder how it would have been to interview Mohammed after his first day of preaching. I'll bet he came back tired, hungry, and discouraged. He probably told his wife "Oh God, everybody hates me, nobody likes me, nobody believes in me, this is going to be a very hard job and some of them even want to lynch me." But obviously that did not stop him; he had a mission to do, and he did it. And Mohammed ended up converting a third of the world.

Many years later the son of one of my father's best friends who had studied to be a doctor in England returned to practice in Trinidad. His father was one of the three founders of The Trinidad Muslim League.

As children we grew up with the Doctor and his siblings but after the falling out between my father and the other leaders of the Mosque we decided to stay away from the Mosque. These religious backbiters had committed the cardinal sin of cutting out my father's picture from a photograph of the three pioneers of The Trinidad Muslim League. The newspapers report documenting the opening of the Mosque in which a photograph of all three pioneers of the Trinidad Muslim League had been taken in anticipation of such an event, published a photograph with our father Hakim Khan obliterated and cut out by those who had stabbed him in the back. My father was betrayed and he felt bewildered and sad. This was a very un-Islamic thing to do, without being told to do so, every one of my father's children boycotted the opening ceremony of the Mosque and to this day we have stayed away from worshiping there. My sister vowed to have that picture restored and the full picture reprinted in every newspaper in Trinidad. She had this done and the crusade ended only when the newspaper gave my father the recognition he deserved for being the hero behind the building of The Jinnah Memorial Mosque which stands a few hundred yards away from our home.

When my sister and I went home on one of our visits we learned that Dr. Feroze would visit my mother often and gave her medical help. To this day he attends to members of my family in Trinidad and he refuses to take money from us for his services. It is an amazing gesture for a man to have such strong feelings for our family since he did not owe us a duty but only friendship-it is not for me to judge but I think he was trying to make atonement for what his father had done to our father. My family is very grateful to him for his kindness and my brothers are still vey close to him. They socialize with him and Nisa thinks he was one of the most remarkable human beings she has ever known. He is a good and caring doctor who is well respected by everyone in the town of St. Joseph. He visits our home often and in fact he was asked to witness my mother's will which he willingly did and all of us love him dearly. And while I am on this subject, I ought to mention another good doctor. I refer to Dr. Michael Pelly who saved the life of Nisa Khan or at least on two occasions. Dr. Pelly is a credit to the medical profession and although he may never have visited Trinidad, he truly deserves a place in this book. Little did Dr. Pelly know that the woman whose life he saved from time to time was actually known throughout the Caribbean as "The Pride of Trinidad"- yes, Nisa Khan is a writer, barrister, Civil Rights activist and lover of beautiful objects of art. Yes- Dr. Pelly the life you saved is one of inestimable value. Sadly, as this manuscript was about to go to the publisher, Dr. Feroze Rafeek passed away. We shall mourn him and we shall all miss him.

Nisa Khan, writer, barrister and human rights campaigner is the daughter of Hakim Khan-first president of the Trinidad Muslim League. A tireless researcher into her family history, Nisa Khan has made a major contribution to this book. She is the sister of this book's author.

Writer/Editor/Lecturer

In addition, my dad had researched books on Ancient Egypt during the time of the Pharaohs and wrote an unpublished story based on one of the great Pharaohs. He also wrote a commentary on Shi Hwanng. He felt, that Shi, who built the Great Wall of China, was the greatest of all Chinese emperors. Although the Trinidad Muslim League was founded in August, 1947, it was twenty years before the Mosque was completed. Twenty years that my dad had to maintain a constant fund-raising effort in order to come up with the money to finally build the mosque. It was truly a tremendous amount of devotion to a singular cause that everyone now appreciates. Prior to the completion of the Mosque, my dad held religious services right in our home because we had a very large home and it could hold many people and feed the poor if they needed a meal.

Because of the bickering and fighting in India itself, my father wrote many articles promoting the unity of all Indians and saying that they should all work together, at least in Trinidad. My dad took some heat because of this from the India Club, but he stuck to his guns and was entirely vindicated later on when his policies became accepted and successful. My father later served on the British Board of Film Censors in the late 1940's, and was one of the founding members and the first president of The Trinidad Muslim League. This was very important because of my father's devotion to education and particularly his belief in more freedom for Muslim women. Under his influence, women were encouraged to attend public lectures and meetings and take part in Bazaars and in social and welfare works. My sister is a product of these reforms, and today she is a writer and barrister in London. Indeed most of the members of my family are business-oriented, independent-minded people.

I feel after all these years that my father was a sensible charmer and, with his good wits, set about doing what I believe was a call from God. He wasn't known world wide, but he was an exceptional and humane person. But just as in the case of Moses who led the Hebrews to the Promised Land but was not allowed by God to enter, my dad did all these wonderful things for his people, yet he was denied this one privilege. My father led the building to completion but just when he was about to go from builder to preacher, he grew ill, giving his life to his project.

Soon after, the Jinnah Memorial Mosque was known far and wide in the island, but the man who people loved for his humanitarianism in this project was not to see the fruits of his labor. However, he gave the Muslim people of St. Joseph and all their descendants, from the diverse cultures of the Far East, Europe and Africa, a place of worship. But his health had deteriorated. He was just one man leading the way. Sadly, my father died in 1957 and never lived to see Trinidad become Independent from Britain in 1962. Mohammed Hakim Khan was not angry but he refused to appear in front of the India Sub-Committee. In his reply to that organization, he defended a journalistic right to freedom of expression. One of his reasons for not appearing in front of the committee was that he was not prepared to be judged by the very same people (acting now as judges) who had accused him of "misconduct" for writing such an article and who were guilty of spreading the wrong words.

On the 7, October, 1946, The India Club decided not to carry out his expulsion, and after stating that the whole incident was regrettable, asked him to "continue to collaborate in carrying out the aims and objects of the club." But they didn't did do this out of sympathy. Surely they had seen my father was selfless and, inevitably, the committee decided that there was no one else to continue the good works that he had started.

The 15th day of August, 1947 saw the birth of the Trinidad Muslim League of which my father, Mohammed Hakim Khan, was the first president. Freedom of expression and of thought, which he so cherished, were just a few of his reforms. Perhaps the most significant reform was the freedom given to the Muslim womenfolk, including his own daughters. Under his influence, they threw off the shackles that had bound women. They soon started to attend public lectures, and meetings and took part in bazaars and other social, cultural, and welfare work. The Trinidad Muslim League offered special thanks to the Pioneers of the League, and my father was not only one of the Pioneers, but indeed "the driving force behind the building of the mosque." The Jinnah Memorial Mosque was opened in 1954.

My Dad's Business

According to Nisa, my father left his safe and secure department store job and decided to go into business. This would have been when he was twenty-five years old and married to Batoolan who was thirteen years old at the time. He struck out on his own confident that he could make a living and support his wife and himself by getting a van and going from town to town selling bolts of cloth to wholesale shops who would in turn sell them to the little vendors, tailors, seamstresses, and others. He was well-liked by his customers, was faithful to them, and he built up his business.

Hakim had been brought up in the house his mother lived in and when he became successful in business, he took over the mortgage and rebuilt the house, for it was an old building. He kept the property in good shape and made sure that there was enough food for all to eat. These responsibilities were the reason why his other brothers and sisters did not inherit the house in St. Joseph. They were all paid cash toward their share of the land and property. My father had the responsibility of a wife and the caring of his parents, while the other family members moved away and lived their own lives. His brothers and sisters had no animosity or anger toward him because of this. He was always respected among them, and they would come to him for advice all the time. Not only did my father take care of his wife and parents, but at times his brothers and sisters came to him with their problems and troubles and asked for his advice.

He never turned his back on any member of his family; he gave them advice, fed them, and if they needed financial help he would give them money. He always had an open house to all, both his family and friends. He always held the same belief that people can change their lives for the better even in times of the worst crisis. From rich to poor all respected him. I have the feeling that my dad not only inherited this value from his ancestors but also was chosen to lead his life by faith and by God. He was a wise man, indeed, and his character showed in the things he did and how graciously he performed them.

My Father's Health and "Tara"

Even though my dad was prosperous in business, his health was failing him and he knew that he was dying, but he did not let my mother know of his ill health. She was fragile with thirteen children to bring up, and she would have been sad and upset. She was too attached to him, not believing that death would intervene. No, they were married at an early age, and she was sure they would grow old together. I do not think that she ever realized that he would leave her. She knew that my father was ailing and that his health was an every-day complaint. What she did not know was that even though his mind was there, his body was breaking down. He didn't complain to my mother because he knew that she would worry and get sad. My mother had all these children to take care of, and the pain of knowing that my father was very sick would cause her more anguish; she would be living in fear. From time to time my dad said to my mother, "This house belongs to the children, you must not sell the house and land. If anything happens to the children, then they will have a place to return to- this home is their security in life."

My father had seen the movie *Gone with the Wind* and he recalled the story of how Scarlet O'Hara, after all the suffering stemming from the Civil War, and with her husband Rhett Butler leaving her, the only hope was to return to the land that her father left her. With nothing left, Scarlet returned to the land and her home, Tara, which was her only hope and the land both she and her father loved very much. Scarlet's return to Tara was symbolic to my dad. No matter what happened, he stressed that our home must remain for the children and that our "Tara" must never be sold and must remain a refuge for the whole family regardless of how much struggle and hardship prevailed in the future. He fought to keep the land and house in hard times. His health was failing; he would not live forever and would not be here to see what would happen. He confessed to my aunt Doris, "I don't think that I will live long. You must help my wife to keep the house." Doris understood the story of Tara in *Gone with the Wind* quite clearly.

Looking back, our forefathers fought and struggled to have land and property after freedom from indentureship and had come a long way from a land of poverty to Trinidad, to sow their seeds and reap the harvest of independence. In our generation, this is what my family and I have been fighting for… to keep our "Tara" at St. Joseph, where my father lived and died.

The Family Members after My father's Death

My mother began drinking when Pa died. She was lonely and turned to friends whenever she came into contact with them. She wanted to console herself by hiding her problems with so many children to care for and no husband to advise her what to do or how to carry on. She was so depressed that she tended to neglect the family at times, as well as neglect the chores. She cried constantly, and the more she drank the more she became somewhat aggressive to her children by scolding them even though she loved all of her children dearly. I, of course, was too young to realize her pain and what she was going through and only now that I am older can I look back and realize what she must have suffered. This woman was helpless, and, with so many responsibilities it was too much for her to cope with. I sometimes think about this and wonder whether I could have done better if I were in her shoes. I doubt it very much. My mother would go to the village markets to buy some food with only a small amount of money, but some of the vendors would give her groceries out of respect, and she, in turn, would greet them with funny stories and jokes and promise to pay them later. But things were getting worse. It was time for my oldest brother to continue my dad's business in order to help in the situation that my mother was facing. In desperation my brother quit his education and took up the reins of my father's business.

Growing up with my mother was mystifying. She told my brothers and sisters stories of her family and how she grew up as a maiden milking cows. She said that her brothers and sisters were so fair that the villagers would say that they had Caucasian blood. She denied being completely Indian for what reason I don't know, but if I can put the pieces right then the puzzle would be solved. She was certainly white as milk and did not follow any particular religion. She said she was of Hindu descent and that her father had died when she was a child. She was indeed a beautiful slender woman with a mole under her lower lip and dark eyes. My father thought that she would be a dutiful wife. She was a worker bee. Just as she milked the cows, her innocence, simplicity and assuring ways were attractive to him. My father was earning a decent wage, and because of her good looks and innocence he asked for her hand in marriage. My father bought her boutique clothes, shoes, and gold jewelry because he admired her and wanted her to look well dressed whenever he took her to banquets and to dances. With her slender build, she looked elegant.

I grew up with a peasant mother who had little education and spoke distinct Urdu and hardly any English. Looking back, I can still see that slender lady caring for so many children, doing the household work hand in hand with the servants. She made the workers feel like residents rather than servants. In the neighborhood, everyone adored her because of her kindness and generosity. She always gave people food and clothing, money and so much laughter that she would be a good comedian even today.

After the death of my father, my mother lamented and vowed that she would never marry again. She just kept on trying to care for us, performing the household duties and always wishing that Hakim was alive. He was in her thoughts daily. I can remember when I was eligible to enter a convent, as the local Catholic high schools were called. Because I had passed the exam to continue my education, and I had the right to go to the closest school, She went to enroll me. She wore a beautiful sari and told the head nun of the convent, "I have lived in this neighborhood for many years, and my husband has passed away. I want my daughter to attend school here and I don't see any reason that she should have to go to another town." She told them that the convent was highly known and she wanted me to have a good education. She could not speak all that much English to convince them, but the way she presented herself was enough to make them accept me. My mother was herself, convincing, and had exercised the argument that she lived only a short distance away from the convent and logically her daughter should attend the neighborhood school.

There are so many more episodes to tell, some of laughter, some of tears but through it all my mother was real. She didn't have to dress like a clown to entertain the common folks, but her ways of dealing with people made them appreciate her good sense of humor. With a household full of growing children, she did a wonderful job, in her own way. When I visited my home, my mother was overwhelmed and cried for joy when she saw me. On my departure, she cried even more and I wept to go back to London. This is indeed a mother who cared for her family and all other people.

As I grew up, my older brother Khalique became our adopted father. He spent years saving the property from being repossessed. After all, he was a young man just out of college and had dreams of his own, but he was thrust into my dad's business without a choice. He made sacrifices to keep our family together and it wasn't easy for him to assume all the responsibilities, in addition to having a mother who had little education and thirteen hungry mouths to be fed.

My brother knew that my father's health was failing; he sensed that this man who was devoting himself to the mosque was neglecting his family and his health. My dad came home exhausted most evenings and many times just went to sleep without eating meals. Why was my father sacrificing his life to a monument, day and night, while neglecting his own family? We can only guess. Overnight, my brother, the carefree young boy, became a man; with my father's passing away, Khalique took on the full responsibilities of providing and taking care of my mother and his younger brothers and sisters.

During Khalique's school vacations, my dad had taught him how to run the business. My father would take him on business trips so that he could meet the customers, and he would deliver their goods in order to acquaint himself with them. My father would talk to him while they traveled to villages to sell, and he fondly remembers the good times they had on business trips. How did my father deal with customers so eloquently and make business progress so rapidly with everyone? I can only say that my dad had a way with words and had good attitude with his customers. My brother was shy and never thought that he would acquire those skills. But he did. It's amazing how adversity can bring out the best in people.

Every cent my brother earned was used to provide food for our family's table. He would remember my dad's words: "Live and work honestly." His big dreams dissolved into a world of hard reality. Seeing my mother with so many children made him work harder by the minute and the hour to earn money. My father loved his wife and children and my brother had the same virtue. Even today, his younger brothers and sisters are like his children and they respect him for all that he has done to bring a family so close together. When Khalique got married, he moved to Tobago and continued his own business there. My younger brother Baita took over the responsibility of the house. His job at the William H. Scott lumber yard allowed him to repair the house and to provide food to the younger children. My mother felt comfortable with this son, and she was always praising him for his devotion to the family. My brother still works at the lumber company and he is admired by his co-workers. There are always pleasant remarks about him by neighbors; his friends admire him with respect and open arms.

My brother Afzal ran the family business while Baita kept the house going. Khalique guided Afzal in selling and taught him how to keep the books in order. Although he had no formal education, Afzal took the business seriously; daily he would drive the van to see customers and deliver the goods. He also went to the Port of Spain wharf to export items to Tobago and import from the smaller island as well in order to sell to the vendors in Trinidad. He is a dutiful and faithful brother. He was similar to Khalique in keeping the business going. He worked all over the island selling his products to earn a salary. The other side of him was that he was also the family gardener and kept the property so beautiful with fruit trees and flowering plants that our house is the envy of the neighborhood. He had some traits like his grandfather Shah and was fond of animals, particularly dogs. Afzal has devoted his life to our home and business, and he has kept the house in its magnificent state.

I will take you back to the oldest member in the family. While my dad's business was still doing quite well, my sister Shannon went to the local French baking school and received a diploma. My father bought her lovely clothes, and she was well groomed. Soon it was time for his eldest daughter to be married. She had met a man whom she knew my dad would accept. He came from a wealthy family and was a gentleman. She was married and moved away with her new husband to set up house. But later, they faced difficult times, and then lost their house.

Before my father's eyes, both my sister and her husband returned to our house. I was a child, but my sister Nisa had told me about our family's ups and downs. My eldest sister, Shannon returned to our home. My father welcomed her and her husband, and she soon gave birth to his first grandson and called him Nizam. My sister's daughter, Sharlene Flores, is currently one of the best folk music singers in Trinidad and with her husband Wayne, performs with their group "Flores de San Jose."

My father loved all his children, but sometimes there is one child who is closer than the others. My sister Zeeni was always at his side. At sixteen, with no academic education, she was at home mostly when he came in after his journey from the mosque. She attended to his needs, and sat close to him at bedtime and cajoled him. Her world revolved around him, and after his death, she felt very alone and alienated herself from my mother and the rest of us.

With no funds, Zeeni was trapped and deprived of education. Later she found a job in a furniture store in Port of Spain, where she met her husband and later had two children. Her mind was still etched with the face of my father, and to this day she recalls his powerful voice, his dedication to his religion, and his devotion to my mother and his children. On reflection, she realizes that my mother was facing a battle with no husband and thirteen mouths to feed. The future seemed not only terrifying but also grim.

The youngest members of my family were my four sisters, Halima, Zalina and Salina (twins) and the youngest child Bebe. My father was gone, and my last sisters cannot recall him except for seeing the family photos on the library mantelpiece of my father and mother looking at each other as if they were newly married. These four missed all of what went on, and now that he was dead, they had no childhood memories of him, only his face and photographs. Friends told us all "Mr. Khan gave his life to his wife, children, and the mosque." He was a courageous and powerful man. One can look back and see his determination and fulfillment in constructing his dream.

My sisters believed what was said of him but reached out for help and guidance from our older brother Khalique. They had no choice, as he had now become their father. Our own father wasn't there for them when they needed him. For years they felt left out, deprived of the father who did not see them grow up, a father who wasn't there to read them bedtime stories. They blamed him for their struggling and lack of education. Later on, as they grew older, they realized that their father, even though he was no prophet, did not make them bitter toward religion or all that he had done for the mosque. Today, they still cherish his memory.

Family Achievements

Some of us earned high degrees and MBEs from Queen Elizabeth College. Some went into the petroleum business, and some owned stores in San Juan. One grandson and his wife made costume designs for the yearly Carnival and for the Miss World Pageant when it was held in Trinidad and Tobago. The author of this book went to London to become a nurse, but ended up earning her living as a model and then came to the US, married, and had two wonderful children.

Chapter 9

BIO OF ZOBI

Zobi

Researcher/Author

I was born in St. Joseph, the old capital of Trinidad, a little island off the coast of South America. Trinidad is famous for sugar, oil and asphalt. It has all the beauty of the other Caribbean islands but in addition has its own natural resources.

My great-great grandfather, Mohammed Moktee, signed a contract with the British East India Company to work in the cane fields for twelve years. I was born the daughter of a local merchant who built his own business and married a beautiful farmer's daughter. Some parents were able to send their children to kindergarten programs for two years prior to entering the school system. Then to primary school from age six to eleven. At age 11 children could enter secondary institutions, whether they were Catholics, Presbyterians, or other religions based on a test. Successful completion of this was determined by a national examination, and those students who passed were allowed to enter the secondary level. Those who failed the examination stayed behind and spent another two years, again trying for the national exam or alternatively, could leave the school system. Four years of academic instructions followed in either a school of their choice or in the vicinity where the students lived. That was how the system worked, and this determined the student's grades at the end of their academic year. After that, many went abroad to further their education in London, Canada, or the United States. Of course, most students simply stayed at home on the island to work for the government or other jobs.

My father made a good living as a businessman, and I attended one of the best Catholic private schools in the island for my secondary education. My mother entertained my classmates after school by making them local delicacies. This was her humble way of being kind to some who lived in village huts and survived with whatever little their parents provided for them. They could not afford to go to street vendors for sweet cakes or sweet drinks. I graduated from the convent school with high marks in history and literature. My school years came to a close, and I graduated with the other students only to see the last of them.

After graduation, I was sent to live with my older sister, who was a lawyer in London. My goal was to become a nurse, but in very short order, found that I could not stand the sight of blood. My sister then enrolled me in a business course so that I could get an office job. I worked at her friend's law office in Knightsbridge. The sights and sounds of London intrigued me. Never in my life had I seen such excitement and energy, double-decker red buses, Buckingham Palace, and even the Queen. The face of the Queen showed on our island's money. All this was so incredible to me. I loved the London museums, walking through Hyde Park, and of course Harrods, the fabulous department store that made me feel like a peacock just to buy a cup of coffee at their restaurant called the Way-Inn. Best of all, on weekends, I would dress up and go out with my friends, dancing in clubs. This became a regular social event. But I always had to be at home early because my sister was very strict.

How I became a Model

Me as a Model

There were not many opportunities to work in Trinidad. After I graduated from St. Joseph's Convent, I asked my family's permission to go to England for the purpose of studying to become a nurse. I knew that I had a sister in England but some of us had not heard from her for many years. It was only later when I was in England I realized she was alone in a strange country struggling to make ends meet. Many other students who went abroad had their families to support them financially whilst they studied for their various professions.

My father had died suddenly a year after her arrival in England, and she was compelled to give up her studies and work for a living, to pay for her accommodation and to support herself. In those days salaries were very, very low. Not being able to send money home, my sister seldom wrote. I think that she may have felt guilty that she was not able to help the family financially at the time. Having said this, once she qualified as a barrister, many years later, she has more than made up for this. Not only did she start sending my mother a regular allowance, but she sent for my two sisters Hal and Bebe and gave them a chance to live and work in England. The low wages in Trinidad meant that they would have had no future in Trinidad and would have stagnated in small office jobs in Port of Spain.

I wasn't in the nursing hospital for long and I was uncomfortable and struggling with this profession. I couldn't go along with this profession much longer and every day was a nightmare just getting up and following the rules and daily agenda. The Matron wrote to my sister to come and take me away because she felt I was unsuitable for the nursing profession. I also felt the same way because I realized that I was not cut out for nursing. I couldn't stand the sight of blood. My sister took me back to London with her and after the first week of sharing her small apartment the landlord rented her another studio for my use.

Many students in England in those days lived in what was called "bedsitting" accommodations. This consisted of one large room, with bathroom and toilet outside and a communal kitchen for those who wanted to prepare meals. We seldom had to cook simply because my sister knew a young man from Tobago who had left the island many years before and had been trained as a chef. George was rather effeminate and was taken under the wings of a noble English "peer of the realm." He catered luncheons for wealthy directors in the city of London, and later on he was asked to cater Prince Andrew's private parties. Many afternoons on his way home he would turn up with ready made portions of the best English and French cuisine which were untouched because of over-supplying meals. George lived in a separate apartment in the building on the third floor. He was not a student, so he could afford to rent a real apartment because he earned good money as an established caterer. It was George who used his contact with wealthy directors who found me my very first job in England, with the Mental Health Association. He had known my sister for many years and she would often give him advice in his quest to buy a home and the ways and means of obtaining a mortgage, etc. Within the first week of my arrival in England my sister had taken me shopping at Harrods to buy warm clothing, etc. Harrods, the largest department store in England, was chosen for the simple reason that it was situated about five hundred yards away from where we lived.

Meanwhile, I would often accompany George at his request to the Playboy Club. He needed a young lady as an escort. For me, George was safe. Like most girls in London who were not attached to any one person I was glad to visit such places. My sister had no objection because she knew George was "gay" and explained that word to me. I would leave George at the gambling table and go off with a few boys who asked me to dance. I enjoyed myself while George had a little flutter in the casino. It was all clean fun and life was pleasant.

London was a very conservative city in the sixties and everyone was having fun from the celebrities to the models and ordinary folks. There was no overt segregation of the races and even if there was, my sister and I were not affected. We lived in Knightsbridge-t he most elite part of London even though we lived in bed dormitories. My sister had made friends with law students, lawyers and some of the staff of the Trinidad and Tobago High

Commission in London with whom she had attended school in Trinidad in their early days. They were school friends from youth and these friendships continued.

This was London in the 1960's- it was different from America where the Civil Rights Movement was gaining momentum. We would read of the black American "activists" like Angela Davis, Martin Luther King. But America was far away and our lives were not affected by segregation. On the contrary, English people were very polite to foreigners and the influx of refugees had not yet begun. In fact, the English were fighting the Irish but this did not mean much to us. We wondered why they fought each other and read about the hunger strikes of the Irish and about Bobby Sands, the martyr who starved himself to death for his cause. He called for peace between England and Ireland. Apart from that, there was no terrorism or war as in the early seventies. London in the sixties will be remembered by all as a fun era, or the swinging sixties. By this time I had made many friends of my own, both males and females and on weekends we would go to discotheques where many celebrities also used to go and to dance and have fun.

After a short spell of working as a typist/receptionist at The Mental Health Association, the boss asked me to leave, but in a very courteous English manner. He told my sister and George that I was spending far too much time out of the office for lunch. I think this was because on reflection now I did not understand the responsibility of having to fend for myself. For example, one had to pay rent to survive and my sister was always there to help. But as time went on I saw my other girlfriends working and taking their jobs, careers, or professions seriously.

One day I was sitting alone in a café and having a breakfast of tea and toast. This was not the best meal I could have but I had little money and was on a budget. The café was half empty and I was there alone thinking about what I could do next. The reflection of my sister saying to me "take a business course which would help you find a job" was on my mind. However, an office job did not seem to stir any emotions with me. Little did I realize that when I was almost finished with my breakfast, in front of me stood a stranger who asked politely if he could join me. As he sat down opposite me he told me that he was a fashion photographer and that he would like to take some pictures of me. He said he thought I would make a really good model. He would also help me to get agency. Was this supposed to be some sort of a joke? Or did he just want to chit chat with a young stranger? I was a bit scared but I wanted to know for what reason he was smiling and paying me such compliments.

Was this true? The pictures would be free and I would have a portfolio ready to start working right away. This man produced a business card and gave it to me. I did not have to say much as he was doing all the talking and I was just listening. I was cautious and somewhat nervous, so I told him about my strict sister and he would have to consult her. That seemed to be no problem to him. After he left I was somewhat surprised and filled with awe. I did not know whether to believe him or not, even though he gave me his business card. The next day my sister got a phone call and without hesitation told me about the photographer. At first she was suspicious, but did not want to stand in my way. My sister was not totally negative but warned me to take precautions if he did not say what he meant. I was actually surprised that my sister said it was o.k. In a week's time, I was having my pictures taken with all clothing and accessories provided by this man's studio. Everything was done as he said and I was elated to know that I could become a model and earn far more money than I imagined. Before I knew what was going on I was sitting in an agent's office and signing up to work for him as a model.

Everything happened so quickly, the photographer knew of a few contacts. My photos (called "headshots") were shown around to several different agencies. Soon I was contacted by an agent named David Mainman of South Kensington who was particularly looking for my type of looks. I signed a contract for one year with my new agent. Soon I became fairly well known to his clients, and I began to get work regularly. In fact, I was one of the first Indian girls from the Caribbean to be accepted as a model in England.

From an island girl to an English model was certainly a big step. Was this fantasy or reality? Modeling was fun and exciting as I strolled through Hyde Park with my portfolio swinging with the wind. I usually took a bus on an assignment but often I would walk to places within reach and often bystanders would call out if I wanted companionship and taxis would pop their horn at me. I looked forward to going on location or having my pictures done in the studio and sometimes wished the day would never end. There were long hours at times in fashion houses filled with all kind of beautiful clothes, shoes and jewelry which I wore to show clients. I was fascinated by all of this glamour. On location, I made friends and hardly ever had a boring moment. This was a good business. I got all types of food and refreshment and all I had to worry about was my bus fare to get home. I can still remember when I got my first paycheck and the look on my sister's face when I was able to help her with the rent.

The photographs changed my whole life. When they were distributed to agencies and fashion houses, my agent got me bookings. I was filled with joy that I could ever be called for one assignment, far more many more. I thought that this change in career might make me a new happy person and also put money in my pockets. I never really looked back at that office job my sister said I should have pursued. My life certainly was changing and I was enjoying every minute as a model with places and faces that I have never forgotten. So my career went on for two years. Taking the bus, underground and sometimes taxis to get me to the job. I was on assignment practically every week, going to the English countryside and sometimes to the continent. I remember my visit to Ibiza (a resort island off the coast of Spain) where I did a photo shoot on a beach cliff and almost fell off the rock. I almost got killed. I begged the photographer to finish as soon as possible because of the danger of getting hurt.

To this day I have never forgotten that stressful assignment. The money on almost all jobs was really good. Sometimes I made the equivalent of $100 an hour or more. Depending on the assignment, I got paid more money for going on location to various places outside of London. I did hair advertisements, book and magazine covers, even photographing my hands and so much more. There was also a feature article in an English newspaper where people of color were moving ahead in the fashion industry. I was becoming a successful model and money was pouring in from all directions. I was making headway and having a good time at what I was doing. The purpose of it all was that I was earning more money that I had ever dreamed of. Back on my island of Trinidad I would have been getting nowhere. But now I was in the pitch of my career. I wanted the best of both worlds. I wanted to achieve a career and still be able to visit my home. I wanted to be that Island girl, and when in London, be an English woman.

I was given much publicity in London and made headlines in Tdrinidad and one of the newspapers wrote that I was "the student nurse who became a model" and claimed that I was earning hundreds of dollars per day. The money I earned was fairly good but not as much as the papers exaggerated. I was kept very busy modeling for fashion houses, magazines, ads, photo shoots from London to the Continent. Once I did a large poster for Italia advertising the Italian National Airline. I had to be passed off as Italian and it worked.

My sister was pleased and proud of my career. She began to take me places like the "Pair of Shoes," a nightclub in the heart of London where the aristocrats dined and gambled. This was hot stuff to be doing. I was dressed to kill and met people there who admired me and asked me out for dates. Now, I was cautious of that kind of life. Eating, drinking and having fun was great, but I was on my guard and stuck to my model girlfriends with whom I felt comfortable. We went out dancing, sightseeing, and to local pubs. It wasn't hard to have boyfriends and I would date the ones I felt that I could trust. It was a kind of instinct that I had. At times, I forgot to keep in touch with my family but when homesickness hit me in the deep corner of my heart I wrote to my mother saying "Ma, I am a small time model but I am making some nice money now" and I am sure she was glad not only to hear from me but to get a few dollars.

My mother even called the neighbors and other relatives and told them how well I was doing in London. After all, she was a widow who depended on one son for supporting my brothers and sisters so I can visualize the tears coming down as she read my letter. My family was excited and having sent them some pictures they even framed them and placed them on the mantelpiece next to my dad. So my life was changed from a sheltered convent girl to a woman in a big time city surrounded by Big Ben, buses and taxis hooting their horns. I moved out of my sister's apartment and shared with a girl friend. The money was coming in and I could pay the rent and besides I wanted to be independent. I loved the crowded streets and Harrods, the famous department store where I would join my friends and have lunch laughing and chatting about all sort of things that had happened. My weight never seemed to be a problem even if I ate as much as I could. I was not steadily employed all the time and when I did not get some jobs I was kind of worried but this did not stop me from trying. I kept doing my daily routine and my agent kept me busy because he could count on me for being on time and without complaints. I was making him good money, too. There were other times when I was not chosen for a job I wanted, and I felt somewhat insecure. I had to worry somewhat and kept on thinking was it the end of my career? Would money be coming in, or was this the end. Was my career over? Or do I have to find another job? But I did not let these thoughts keep me back or get me depressed. Something always came up and I knew this was the name of the game in modeling.

Other models kept dieting and struggling to keep in shape. Some models were afraid of going out in the sun. Looks mattered in this profession, so some models kept on a starvation diet, even a hot dog or some French fries were too much to eat. Others would buy loads of cosmetics to keep their face from wrinkling. Some stayed out of the sun and wore sun glasses and sun lotions for fear of losing their looks. I had heard enough from some of my friends who said "I could not do this or could not do that because it was bad for my image." I had heard or seen enough and I was glad that my color did not pull me away from work, but was actually an advantage. Two years of modeling and that was a lot of time, dating handsome men and meeting other famous models. Far from it all, I was lucky and had good health, which kept me on the move.

I was going to places all over London looking good and keeping my assignments on time. For print work in studios, I often got my clothes and accessories free. I never had a dull moment. The whole affair was a wonderful game. I loved it and played it well.

Other "black" models came on the scene and I knew the time had come for me to make a move. I realized it was too late to start a new profession in England. It was two years well spent in modeling but now I could not see a future for me in England. After a few years I wanted to visit my sister in the US who was having her first baby. They invited me to come and stay with them and I took advantage of the opportunity, accepted the invitation and went to America. But I did not like what I had seen of my sister's life in America. In a way, I regretted leaving London and my sister and the easy comfortable life I had there. I missed going to the theatre, the museum and all those other wonderful places. I found the culture in America very strange. I had to get away from the environment of my sister and her husband, who kept arguing all day and night. My sister Nisa was living like a civilized and cultured English lady. She did not argue or fight with her very prim and proper friends.

Is this the American dream I asked myself? I must get out and do something constructive. I had left England to make a better life. Only a few weeks after my arrival, I met a young blond man who took me out to dinner after his working hours. His apartment was a sort of sanctuary for me to get away from where I was living. This man, Gary, would become my husband and this was fate. He offered to walk me home. He was quiet and worked hard for a living. Within a few weeks, Gary asked me suddenly out of the blue to marry him. I quickly said "yes" because I could not see the idea of spending any more time at my sister's place. Gary was a printer at a well known New York company and although he was not wealthy he earned a fairly good living. We got married and I was glad because it meant the end of immigration problems as I had come to the US as a visitor.

I exchanged my ticket and did not return to London. My agent in London was furious. I gave up my glamorous career in London to settle down and raise a family in New Jersey. I looked for work but I could not find any model agencies in New York that would accept me. My type of nationality was not needed in these agencies, they said. They were not used to colored models at that time, no matter how good my looks were. I decided to try some secretarial agencies to find work to keep me going. Soon after, I found a job as a receptionist and carried on working. Soon I had two children. The years passed and by this time we had bought a home and we made sure the children were given a good education. I kept on working while I raised the children.

My two children had the advantages of a nice house in the suburbs, good schooling, a picket fence, two cars and two dogs. I settled into family life. When the children got older I got a job in an office where I worked for eight years. When the factory closed, I wanted another job but something more exciting than the boring routine of office work. A friend suggested that modeling or acting might still be a good career for me, so I enrolled in the local community college for a semester in drama. After the course ended, I had headshots (photos) taken and I began to look for work. I went into New York City to take acting classes at HB Studios in Greenwich Village for two years. Soon, I was called for bit parts in films, television, commercials, fashion shows, background and print jobs. These included *One True Thing, The Siege, Sopranos, A Mercedes Benz Commercial, HBO video, Saturday Night Live and more.*

Conclusions

I think there should be a lot more effort by East Indians to publish their experiences in books and magazines. All too often, East Indians are mistaken by Americans to be a different race, that is, African -American, American Indian, Arab, Hawaiian or other ethnicities, and not recognized to be their own distinct group. If we support ourselves and speak up for what we believe, I think that we can encourage our people and promote our culture, in television and movies, in more positive roles. The negative stereotypes we are accustomed to, such as being portrayed as terrorists and war-like people, crazed by religious fanaticism and by wars and conflicts that make no particular sense to American people, give a very negative impression of the rich culture that India has going back thousands of years. The negative stereotypes actually affect all of us, because they shape public opinion of our community in the United States.

I feel our role should be to let the public know that we have thousands of years of culture, with many exciting and interesting things in our history. I realize that it is money that determines which pictures, movies, books, and magazine get made. Publishers are similar to Hollywood movie studios in that the bottom line is what really counts. An executive always looks to see how a previous project has been done before deciding to sign up another project. So, if they get the feeling that the communities that they are going to portray in a book or movie does not support their own people, in their own project, these executives are less likely to gamble on this topic. Not taking risks means that East Indians get represented once again as in their stereotypes that are warlike, hostile, religious fanatics, and terrorists. East Indian people should be more supportive of the accurate and truthful descriptions of our community…our culture, our love, and our proud history. Of course, it might help if more young Indian people were encouraged to go into the arts, film, publishing, and to books, and theater. Many would be able to pursue their dreams. If they were encouraged to do some of this, it would certainly go a long way toward educating the American public about Indian culture, Indian practices, Indian history, and the wonderful, rich background that Indians have to offer. It is true that commercials, entertainment, movies, books, films, and theater today portray all different ethnicities and races. The men and women who are shown are in good shape and current styles, and are active both physically and mentally. All other ethnic types are used in advertising, in commercials and in theater, but our culture does not stand out in this field. We are homogenized into American culture or portrayed as some other ethnic group.

We must not be represented as terrorists any longer. Indians are people with a long and rich culture. This will come out some day sooner or later. There is a tremendous amount of history, passion, color and many dynamic things that have happened, all having to do with the Indian culture.

There are many wonderful stories to tell, certainly at least as wonderful as all those tales of European knights in their shining armor, all the fables of kings and queens and the rich history of Europe and Western culture. How many American people really know who built the Taj Mahal and why? It is such a fascinating tale. There is an equal amount of culture, history, pageantry, love, war, and color to be had from the Indian sub-continent as there is from any other area of the globe.

Until now Indians have often been represented as other races, such as American Indians, Haitians, Caribbean and Arabs. This could easily be changed, and the public would be happy to hear of it. We have so much culture to offer, it is truly amazing that our history and background have been such an undiscovered "diamond in the rough." I feel strongly that we will one day come to a point where Indians are equally represented. Something tells me that consumers will see what is happening and will come to love and enjoy stories of Indian culture, like any other stories of Western culture. Books will be written and movies will be made. I can see this happening. Equal attention and better opportunities for Indians are just around the corner. I know that with our background of hard work and dedication, education, and self-reliance, the message will become clear, that is: we can do anything that we set our minds to do.

I feel strongly that the public will come to a point where they see that we are equally qualified. Something tells me that as the years go on, here in the US both consumers and industries will see changes happening and the public going for it and our dreams will be fulfilled. Yes, I can see that happening, equal attention and better opportunities are just around the corner and with our background of hard work, quite a number of changes will occur in the next century. This book is exciting, passionate, real, and traces my family roots from poverty in India to independence and prosperity in Trinidad. Research on my book has taken me full circle now back to my home in Trinidad and to my sister in London.

This story is largely set in America and should be unfolded now. I have tried to make the story alive, inspirational and full of human kindness.

END

Printed in Great Britain
by Amazon